This book is to be returned on or before
the last date stamped below.

JEAVONS, P. M.

D1615377

# PHOTOSENSITIVE EPILEPSY

# Photosensitive Epilepsy

A review of the literature
and a study of 460 patients

PETER M. JEAVONS
and
GRAHAM F. A. HARDING

1975

Spastics International Medical Publications

LONDON: William Heinemann Medical Books Ltd.

PHILADELPHIA: J. B. Lippincott Co.

ISBN 433 17201 0

Printed in England at THE LAVENHAM PRESS LTD., Lavenham, Suffolk

*In memory of Dr. James H. Margerison,
staunch friend, scientific critic, and
champion of all those who suffer with
epilepsy*

## Acknowledgements

This study would not have been possible without the co-operation of the 460 patients and their families, many of whom have attended for a number of long and detailed investigations. We are most grateful to them and hope that our investigations have helped them to enjoy life to a greater extent.

Many colleagues have co-operated with us. We would like to thank the numerous consultants who have allowed us to investigate their patients, and the numerous co-workers who have materially contributed to these studies. Some of our co-workers were studying for post-graduate degrees and parts of these studies were included in their theses, under our supervision. We would like to acknowledge in particular Dr. B. D. Bower, Dr. M. Dimitrakoudi, Mr. N. Drasdo, Miss C. Herrick, Dr. M. Kabrisky, Dr. M. C. Maheshwari, Dr. C. P. Panayiotopoulos and Mrs. K. Peace.

For their skilled help we are grateful to our EEG technicians, in particular Cathy Barry, Lee Downey, Kietha Head, Elaine Quinn, Diane Roden and Ursel Trilloe. The staff of the Applied Psychology Workshop have given us the benefit of their electronic expertise on many occasions, and we wish to thank Peter Bailey and John Lindley in particular.

The photographs were produced by the Department of Medical Illustration at the Children's Hospital and the Visual Aids Department at Aston, and we are grateful to David Drury and Roger Banks, and to Lorraine Riddington for preparing many of the graphs and diagrams.

The statistical evaluation was made by Dr. J. A. Waterhouse, to whom we express our thanks. We are indebted to Miss C. Herrick for the analysis of the data for the reliability of limits and for the seven-year prognosis.

We gratefully acknowledge the generous financial support received over the years from the Research Committee of the Birmingham Regional Hospital Board, The British Epilepsy Association, The National Research Development Corporation, and Reckitt and Colman Ltd., who also supplied 'Epilim' (sodium valproate).

We are grateful to our secretaries, Jacky Brown and Carol Krčmár, for their tolerance, and to Margaret Geddes and Carol Krčmár for typing the manuscript. We should like to thank Dr. B. D. Bower for reading it and for his helpful suggestions.

Finally, we apologise to our families for the inconvenience we have caused them in the course of producing this monograph.

P.M.J.
G.F.A.H.

# Contents

# PART II STUDY OF 460 PATIENTS AND 29 RELATIVES

# Part I

# Review of the Literature

CHAPTER 1

# Introduction and Clinical Aspects

**Introduction**

Epilepsy is said to occur in 0.5 per cent of the population, irrespective of the country of origin, since similar figures of incidence are quoted throughout the world. The incidence may be as high as 0.8 per cent in children aged 5-14 (Pond *et al.* 1960, Cooper 1965, Rutter *et al.* 1970). The diagnosis of epilepsy is not always accurate and it is possible that the figure of 0.5 per cent is too high. Twenty per cent of 'epileptic' patients referred to special clinics (Jeavons 1972) and 20 per cent of patients said to have epilepsy studied in a survey of psychiatric hospitals (Betts, personal communication 1974) were found not to be suffering from epilepsy. It is even more difficult to estimate the incidence of various types of epilepsy because of variations in classification, a difficulty not yet overcome, and in some cases accentuated, by international committees (Gastaut 1970, 1973). In this monograph, for example, we shall refer to myoclonic jerks, rather than to 'bilateral massive epileptic myoclonus' (Gastaut 1973) as recently suggested. The 'international' classification and terms are put in parenthesis on the first occasion of the mention of the type of seizure.

The proportions of cases seen at the epilepsy clinics of one of the authors (P.M.J.) are shown in Table I. Inevitably this is a biased sample, especially in view of his known interests (infantile spasms and photosensitivity), but it is possible that there are in general more photosensitive patients than those with true petit mal absences. During the past 12 years about 450 patients have been referred from the Birmingham region where the population is about 5 million. Obviously we have not

**TABLE I**

Convulsion clinic cases: patients divided according to type of seizure
(all figures are percentages)

| Type of seizure | % | International classification* |
|---|---|---|
| Infantile spasms | 8 | Infantile spasms |
| Febrile convulsions | 6 | Febrile convulsions |
| Myoclonic/astatic | 3 | Myoclonic-atonic seizures |
| Petit mal absences | 5 | Typical absences |
| Photosensitive epilepsy | 8 | Visual reflex epilepsy |
| Myoclonic jerks | 3 | Bilateral massive epileptic myoclonus |
| Tonic-clonic | 28 | Tonic-clonic |
| Temporal lobe | 23 | Partial epilepsy with complex symptomatology |
| Focal motor | 6 | Partial epilepsy with motor symptoms |
| Mixed types | 10 | |

*Although the authors do not subscribe to this classification the terms are given for the sake of completeness (Refs: Gastaut 1970, 1973).

3

seen all cases, but the above figures suggest an incidence of photosensitive epilepsy of 1:10,000. Of 14,000 unselected consecutive cases referred for EEG examination at Dudley Road Hospital, 2 per cent were found to show 3 c.sec spike and wave discharges on intermittent photic stimulation (IPS), a figure similar to that reported in France by Gastaut *et al.* (1958).

The present study arose from the work on convulsions and television-viewing reported from the Children's Hospital, Birmingham by Pantelakis, Bower and Jones in 1962. Their study raised a number of theoretical questions, and a study of the literature revealed that hypotheses were numerous, but scientific method was frequently lacking. What was originally planned as a small survey became progressively larger and more complicated, and up to January 1974, 489 patients or relatives were examined in greater or lesser degree. From the point of view of statistical evaluation we are reporting on the first 300 patients, but otherwise all other aspects relate to all 460 patients. The number involved in each study is as follows:

| Study | Number of cases | Year study began |
|---|---|---|
| EEG including photic stimulation | 489 | 1961 |
| Statistical study | 300 | 1962 |
| Sensitivity limits | 292 | 1965 |
| Monocular stimulation | 244 | 1965 |
| Analysis and computation of EEG | 8 | 1967 |
| Spectacles | 22 | 1968 |
| Occipital spikes and VEP | 100 | 1969 |
| Patterns and IPS | 10 | 1970 |
| Effect of lateral gaze | 91 | 1971 |
| Effect of lateral illumination | 52 | 1971 |
| Effect of coloured IPS | 16 | 1972 |
| Photosensitive families | 17 | 1973 |
| Effect of sodium valproate | 23 | 1973 |

**Clinical literature before 1940**

It is the fashion when reviewing the literature relating to epilepsy to quote from classical sources, and thus many authors attribute the first reference to photosensitive epilepsy to Apuleius, in his book 'Apologia' written about 125 AD. Thus it has been stated that 'rotating a potter's wheel might provoke a fit', and that 'this was the earliest recorded association of fits with flickering light' (Mawdsley 1961), that 'an epileptic had a seizure when a potter's wheel was rotated in front of his eyes' (Brausch and Ferguson 1965), that a 'flickering light stimulus was produced by rotating a potter's wheel before the eyes of slaves' (Troupin 1966, Harley *et al.* 1967).

Panayiotopoulos (1972) pointed out that these romantic accounts are not supported by the original translation of the speech made by Apuleius when defending himself against an accusation of practising magic on a young slave, Thallus. The boy had fallen down in front of Apuleius and this was believed to be sorcery. Apuleius said that the boy had epilepsy, which was the cause of his collapse. The relevant quotation

4

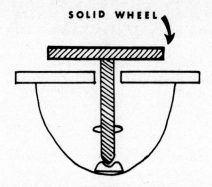

**SOLID WHEEL**

**Fig. 1.** Diagramatic illustration of the type of potter's wheel used in the time of Apuleius. The solid wheel and spindle are cross-hatched.

is as follows:

> 'Again the spinning of a potter's wheel will easily infect a man suffering from this disease with its own giddiness. The sight of its rotations weakens his already feeble mind, and the potter is far more effective than the magician for casting epileptics into convulsions.'
> (Apuleius, Butler's translation, 1909)

There is no mention of flickering light, and to obtain such a stimulus from a potter's wheel, this would have to be spoked. There is no evidence that spoked wheels were in use at the time (Cook, personal communication 1970) and it appears that spoked wheels were not used until the 13th century (Rieth 1960). The wheel used in the time of Apuleius was of the type shown in Figure 1. The myth about the potter's wheel is but one of the myths associated with photosensitive epilepsy, others being that fits occur in *drivers* of cars travelling along tree-lined roads, that red flashing light is more provocative than white light, and that sensitivity is greater with the eyes closed than with them open.

The first reliable reference to photosensitive epilepsy is that of Gowers (1885) who described a girl who had attacks when going into bright sunshine, and a man who had a visual aura of bright blue lights, his aura and subsequent fit being evoked by looking at a bright light. Radovici *et al.* (1932) described a patient who induced fits in himself using light and Goodkind (1936) reported a method of inducing fits in a photosensitive patient using sunlight. It is interesting that the method involved sunlight coming through a wire window screen, and pattern may therefore have been a factor. Although Adrian and Matthews (1934) described the effect of intermittent photic stimulation (IPS) on the electroencephalograph (EEG), there were no clinical references to photosensitive epilepsy until Cobb (1947) reported the influence of flickering light as a precipitant of fits. The widespread use of IPS as an activating technique dates from the introduction of an electronic stroboscope by Walter *et al.* (1946).

The first report of epileptic fits being evoked by watching television was made by Livingston in 1952, and since that time more than a hundred cases have been documented in the English, French and American literature, the largest group consisting of 35 patients described by Gastaut *et al.* (1960). Subsequently Gastaut and Tassinari (1966) gave some information about a further 27 cases. Amongst the authors describing 'television' epilepsy are Rao and Prichard (1955), Ismay (1958), Klapatek (1959), Richter (1960), Lagergren and Hansson (1960), Pallis and Louis (1961), Mawdsley (1961), Bickford and Klass (1962), Pantelakis *et al.* (1962), Bower (1963), Forster and Campos (1964), Charlton and Hoefer (1964), Jeavons *et al.* (1966) and Hishikawa *et al.* (1967).

**Classification**

Bickford *et al.* (1953) divided their photosensitive epileptic patients into three classes:

a. A clinically sensitive group in which light of the intensity encountered in daily life was capable of inducing clinical attacks;

b. A less sensitive group in which clinical seizures could only be induced under conditions of high intensity illumination and rapid flicker which can be produced in the laboratory;

c. A group in which the only evidence of sensitivity was the occurrence of seizure discharge in relation to stimulation by light unaccompanied by any detectable evidence of seizure.

Doose *et al.* (1969b) also divided their patients into three groups, giving the name 'photogenic' epilepsy to those who had fits only with flickering light, whilst those who had fits without any light stimulus but who showed a photoconvulsive response (PCR) during IPS were called 'photosensitive'. Their third group had photogenic and spontaneous seizures. (We agree with Gastaut *et al.* (1963) that the term 'photogenic' is best reserved for use as a descriptive adjective relating to well-endowed girls and photography).

**Factors Precipitating Fits**

*Sunlight*

Flickering sunlight seen when travelling along an avenue of trees, or past railings, has been reported as a precipitant of fits by many authors (Cobb 1947, Gastaut *et al.* 1948, Walter and Walter 1949, Livingston and Torres 1964).

Walter (1961) quotes a letter from someone who experienced violent movements when sitting in an Army vehicle being driven through an avenue of trees. On a second occasion the same experience occurred, but not if the correspondent looked straight ahead.

It is of interest that Ames (1971) had two patients who did not get photosensitive attacks when driving a car. One patient 'blinked and jerked when being driven in a car along a tree-lined avenue but never if she was the driver'. Jeavons *et al.* (1971) expressed the view that drivers of cars would not get fits under these circumstances because lateral illumination does not evoke abnormal discharges in the EEG during IPS (see page 77).

Sunlight shining through the leaves of trees may be a precipitant (Gastaut and Tassinari 1966), and the interruption of light by the blades of a helicopter has caused

6

fits (Johnson 1963, Gastaut and Tassinari 1966). Bickford *et al.* (1953) and Gastaut and Tassinari have reported patients whose fits were induced by sunlight reflected from snow or the waves of the sea.

*Artificial light sources other than television*

Gastaut and Tassinari (1966) reported fits evoked by oscilloscopes and the blades of a mechanical saw. The flicker of the cinema screen was reported to be a factor by Holmes (1927), and Brausch and Ferguson (1965) had a patient whose fits were induced by fluorescent lighting. The commonest source of artificial flickering light, however, is the television screen.

*Television*

Livingston (1952) postulated that seizures occurring whilst watching television were provoked by television sets which were defective and therefore flickered, or in which the vertical hold was faulty, causing the picture to roll.

In most of the cases subsequently reported in the literature the attacks were said to have occurred either when the patient was watching a faulty set, or was adjusting the set, or was very near to the set. Pantelakis *et al.* (1962) divided their patients into two groups. The very sensitive group tended to have fits when the television set was working properly and when they were viewing at a normal distance, while the less sensitive group had fits when the set was faulty or they were close to it. These authors reported that 9 of their 14 cases had fits only when watching television—Gastaut *et al.* (1960) also found 9 such cases out of their 35 cases of 'television epilepsy'.

Bower (1963) and Charlton and Hoefer (1964) suggested that viewing from an angle might be a factor, and Gastaut *et al.* (1960) listed a number of factors which might have acted as precipitants in addition to the flicker of T.V. These factors included tiredness, influenza, alcohol, premenstrual state and watching jerky cartoons or the interval patterns. Bickford and Klass (1962) suggested that fits induced by T.V. viewing were due to sensitivity to geometric patterns. Patterns, especially black and white geometric ones, are known to induce clinical fits and abnormalities in the EEG (Bickford *et al.* 1953, Bickford and Klass 1962, Bickford and Klass 1969, Chatrian *et al.* 1970).

Gastaut and Tassinari (1966) suggested that fits in television-sensitive patients were induced by the slow, accidental and exceptional frequencies seen by the subject when near to the set in a dimly lit room. Pantelakis *et al.* (1962) suggested three reasons for fits being more common when the patient was close to the set. First, because a larger area of the retina was stimulated, secondly because the periphery of the retina would be involved to a greater extent, and thirdly, because the line details could be seen. The flicker frequency of the picture when viewed from several feet away is 50 per second, whereas if the viewer is near enough he will see individual lines and receive two stimuli each at 25 per second, but out of phase. Bower (1963) and Troupin (1966) pointed out that the rarity of 'television' epilepsy in the United States as compared with Europe may be due to the difference in the mains A.C. frequency, 50 Hz in Europe and 60 Hz in the U.S.A. This results in the two half scans producing flicker at 25 c.sec. in Europe and at 30 c.sec. in the United States, and they stated that more patients with television epilepsy were sensitive to 25 c.sec. than to 30 c.sec.

Several authors have recorded the EEG while the patient looked at a television screen. Gastaut *et al.* (1960) failed to elicit EEG abnormality while their patients viewed television. Richter (1960) and Dumermuth (1961) found that abnormality occurred when the T.V. picture was faulty or when channels were switched. Bickford and Klass (1962) used coloured lights and patterns on a T.V. screen to elicit abnormality in the EEG. Andermann (1971) described a patient in whom switching the set or adjusting a faulty vertical hold induced spike and wave activity which was not present when the set was functioning normally.

The most convincing report is that of Binnie *et al.* (1973) who found, in 10 patients with abnormal responses to IPS, that viewing a domestic television set evoked photoconvulsive responses in 9 of the patients when the set was functioning normally, and that abnormality could be evoked at a greater distance from the set in 5 when the vertical or horizontal hold was faulty. They suggest that the failure of Gastaut *et al.* (1960) to elicit abnormality could have been due to the fact that the equipment provided by Radio Télévision Francaise was of unusually high quality.

Darby and Hindley (1974) reported on 26 patients of whom 10 gave a history of television epilepsy. Twenty-five of the patients showed photoconvulsive responses while watching a domestic T.V. set in the laboratory. The viewing distances varied from 0.5 to 4 m. Increasing contrast or brightness had little effect but interfering with horizontal or vertical hold caused a PCR in 10 patients at distances from which normally-functioning sets had no effect.

The findings of Binnie *et al.* (1973) and Darby and Hindley (1974) of the provocative nature of a faulty picture might support the hypothesis of Livingston (1952). However, it is probable that the most important factor inducing fits is the large area of retina which is stimulated when the individual goes near to the set to adjust the fault. But a faulty picture does present a more contrasing flickering pattern, which could explain the findings of Binnie *et al.* and Darby and Hindley.

Gastaut and Tassinari (1966) summarised the characteristic features of television-induced seizures as arising essentially but not exclusively in children, being almost exclusively of grand mal type, sometimes preceded by myoclonic jerks, and almost always showing spike and wave or polyspike and wave discharges on IPS.

*Self-induced epilepsy*

This appears to be the rarest form of photosensitive epilepsy. The first case was reported by Radovici *et al.* (1932), and Andermann *et al.* (1962) reported 20 cases and reviewed 31 previously described in the literature. Of the 51 cases 35 were female and 15 male (ratio 2:1). Subsequently two cases each have been reported by Chao (1962), Keith (1963) and Wadlington and Riley (1965), 3 by Loiseau and Cohadon (1962), 4 by Harley *et al.* (1967), 7 by Ames (1971) and 9 by Green (1966). Single cases have been reported by a number of other authors, bringing the total to approximately 100.

In this form of epilepsy the patient usually stares at a source of bright light, commonly the sun, and waves one hand with outspread fingers rapidly across the eyes. Some patients are said to stare at bright light and blink rapidly. Ames (1971) in a study of 'self-induced' epilepsy reported EEG abnormality when the patient was asked to blink in sunlight in only one of 6 patients, and EEG abnormality on hand-waving in 2 of 3 patients. Livingston and Torres (1964) suggested that the movement of the hand could be part of the ictus rather than being a voluntary movement, and Hutt (personal communication 1973) has shown that the EEG abnormality preceded the hand movement when both were recorded simultaneously. Ames (1971) also regarded the hand waving as part of the ictus, mainly on the basis of clinical history and cine films of the attacks. Her Case 7 appears to be entirely different from cases usually regarded as being self-induced, in that the patient had continuous myoclonus, ataxia and mental subnormality and was, therefore, presumably suffering from a degenerative disorder. In a later paper (Ames 1974) there is further evidence that the hand-waving was part of the ictus. Many of the patients who induce their fits are said to be of limited intelligence.

Gastaut and Tassinari (1966) claim to have been the first to describe this condition and state that the induced attacks are always absences. However, generalised fits with loss of consciousness with or without incontinence have been reported by Chao (1962), Andermann et al. (1962), Harley et al. (1967) and Ames (1971). Absences, fluttering of the eyelids and myoclonic jerking are all commonly reported as induced fits. Robertson (1954) and Hutchison et al. (1959) reported that the patients appeared to get some satisfaction from the procedure, and this opinion has been expressed by subsequent authors. Hutchison et al. also reported that 15 flashes per second was the frequency of photic stimulation most effective in inducing abnormal discharges, and that this rate could be achieved by hand-waving. Troupin (1966) also suggested that the rate of stimulation achieved by hand-waving is between 1 and 15 per second. Although sunlight is the light source usually used by these patients, Harley et al. (1967) and Andermann (1971) have each reported a patient who used the television screen as a flickering light source; one patient altered the controls to make a blurred image and a rolling picture.

**Types of fit**

Various types of fit may be induced by flickering light, but the commonest is a generalised tonic-clonic seizure, perhaps preceded by myoclonic jerking. A tonic-clonic seizure is certainly the most frequent type of fit induced by television.

Gastaut et al. (1960) reported that a third of their patients had tonic-clonic fits and others became pale and fell. The precise nature of the fit was not known in about a third of their cases, although it was probably tonic. Only one patient had a psychomotor fit, two had focal motor fits and 3 had myoclonic fits. Charlton and Hoefer (1964) described their patients' fits as being either tonic-clonic or confusional episodes; the patients reported by Hishikawa et al. (1967) had tonic-clonic or myoclonic fits alone or in combination. Tonic-clonic fits predominated in the series of photosensitive patients reported by Ganglberger and Cvetko (1956) and Wadlington and Riley (1965).

**Age**

The ages of patients with photosensitive epilepsy reported in the literature range from 5 to 52 years, though Capron (1966) found abnormal discharges during photic stimulation in a child of 2 years and 3 months. However, this child had gross cerebral lesions. Capron stated that the onset of photosensitivity was rare before the age of 5 years, and most commonly occurred between 6 and 12. Most of the patients reported in the literature are below the age of 30 and the condition appears to be most common below 16 years. Gastaut *et al.* (1960) found a mean age of 19.2 years.

## Sex

Many authors do not mention the sex of their patients, but of the 148 patients whose sex is given 64 per cent were female. Doose *et al.* (1969a) found a significantly higher incidence of photosensitivity in the female siblings of photosensitive probands, and Doose *et al.* (1969b) found that photosensitivity was commoner in females. These authors define 'photosensitive epilepsy' as the occurrence of photoconvulsive (spike and wave) response to IPS without any clinical precipitation of fits by flicker, distinguishing it from 'photogenic epilepsy' in which there are fits precipitated by flicker encountered in everyday life. A number of other authors report a higher incidence of abnormalities on photic stimulation in females than males (Herrlin 1954, Melsen 1959, Watson and Marcus 1962, Wadlington and Riley 1965, Troupin 1966).

## Family history

In 1951 Daly and Bickford reported identical twins aged 42 who were photosensitive and whose fits had started at the age of 9 years. Although both showed spike and wave discharges during photic stimulation, their responses were not identical. Davidson and Watson (1956) and Watson and Davidson (1957) found light-sensitivity in asymptomatic relatives of photosensitive patients and regarded light sensitivity as a manifestation of diffuse neuronal disease with a hereditary background. Of four pairs of identical twins, two seemed particularly sensitive to light and relatively insensitive to hyperventilation, and the other two showed the reverse. These authors found that, in 62 per cent of cases, one or more members of the family of the light-sensitive patients showed a photoconvulsive response. Some of these relatives had fits for the first time in their lives when exposed to photic stimulation. Watson and Marcus (1962) found a high percentage of 'photogenic cerebral electrical abnormalities' in the 146 asymptomatic relatives of 60 propositi (50 per cent mothers, 17 per cent fathers, 45 per cent siblings, 32 per cent offspring). It should be noted, however, that five types of EEG abnormality were included in their classification, and only one of these was clearly a PCR (i.e. spikes or spikes and wave), and separate figures for this type of abnormality were not given.

Schwartz (1962) gave details of a family of six, of whom the father, two girls and two boys had EEG abnormalities on photic stimulation, three having fits and two experiencing sensations of 'jumpiness' when exposed to flicker in everyday life. Only the mother had a normal EEG and was entirely asymptomatic. Daly *et al.* (1959) reported a family in whom three members showed photosensitivity, but also had spastic paraparesis and mental retardation. They suggested that sensitivity to light could result from diffuse neuronal disease or stem from a defect in the subcortical systems. Haneke (1963) described a girl with photogenic epilepsy whose mother and sister showed EEG abnormality during IPS and whose grandmother was probably

10

photosensitive. Gerken *et al.* (1968) and Doose *et al.* (1969a) have reported on the hereditary aspects of photosensitivity (by which they mean the abnormalities induced by IPS, as compared to light-induced fits which they call 'photogenic'). These authors found that 26.2 per cent of all siblings showed a PCR compared with 6.7 per cent of controls, and that photosensitivity was markedly age-linked, positive findings occurring in 40 per cent of the children aged 5 to 8 years and 34.5 per cent of those aged 13 to 16 years. The morbidity of seizures was greatest in the female family members, particularly on the maternal side. These authors concluded that 'the PCR is a symptom of a very widespread genetically-determined susceptibility to convulsions of the "centrencephalic" type'.

Chatrian *et al.* (1970) reported two brothers with pattern-sensitive epilepsy, who had photoconvulsive responses on IPS and in response to patterns. The EEGs of their parents and two brothers were normal.

## Summary

In summary, photosensitivity may manifest itself as a laboratory finding in a patient who has epilepsy, or may be associated with the provocation of fits by flickering light stimuli encountered in everyday life. Examples of the latter are television, sunlight reflected off wet surfaces or through leaves of trees, or seen when the subject is moving rapidly past trees or railings illuminated by sunlight shining from the side. Less commonly black and white or sharply contrasted linear patterns may precipitate fits.

The commonest precipitant appears to be television, and the fit is usually a tonic-clonic one. The onset of photosensitive epilepsy is usually below the age of 20 years and females are more affected than males. Television epilepsy is more common in countries where the frequency of the A.C. mains is 50 Hz. There is evidence of a genetic factor in photosensitive epilepsy.

# CHAPTER 2

# Laboratory Studies—Photic Stimulation Factors

It is difficult to evaluate and compare the findings in the literature relating to intermittent photic stimulation (IPS) because of the wide variation in the techniques and the frequent lack of detailed information. Information about techniques of photic stimulation is scanty, and sometimes inaccurate, in all the EEG textbooks.

**Stroboscope and photostimulators**

The first method of IPS was described by Adrian and Matthews (1934) who used a disc with cut-out sectors rotating in front of a car headlight bulb. This produced flicker at rates up to 25 flashes per second (f.sec). Disc-type photostimulators were also used by Daly and Bickford (1951) and Ulett and Johnson (1958).

Walter *et al.* (1946) were the first to use a 'high power stroboscope' which they said had the advantage of producing flashes up to rates of 100 per second. Electronic stroboscopes, or photostimulators, have subsequently been widely used. Most gas-discharge lamps produce a blue-white flash of duration between 10 and 30 $\mu$sec. The parameters of the photostimulators vary and comparison between lamps is very difficult because of the various terms and methods used. A method of measuring the output of photostimulators has been described by Jeavons *et al.* (1972a) and is given in Chapter 7. Most photostimulators will deliver flashes at rates up to 50 per second, and others at rates up to 100 per second. Some photostimulators can deliver double flashes with a variable interval between each flash, and with some it is possible to trigger the photostimulator from one channel of the patient's EEG. The lamps of the photostimulators show considerable variation in size and shape (most are round, but at least one is oblong), in some the bulb is visible, in others there is a diffuser, and in one there is a protective metal grid. These variations in photostimulators add further to the problem of comparing and evaluating the findings of various authors, since all these parameters affect the response of the patient to IPS.

**Frequency**

The flash rates used have varied from 1 to 50 f.sec. and the optimum rates to induce PCR have been found to be between 10 and 25 f.sec., most authors finding a peak of sensitivity between 15 and 20 f.sec. (Walter and Walter 1949, Carterette and Symmes 1952, Bickford *et al.* 1953, Rao and Prichard 1955, Gastaut *et al.* 1960, Kooi *et al.* 1960, Pallis and Louis 1961, Troupin 1966, Jeavons *et al.* 1966, Cooper *et al.* 1969, Kooi 1971). Very few authors test at rates faster than 30 per second (Melsen 1959, Pallis and Louis 1961, Gastaut *et al.* 1962, Pantelakis *et al.* 1962, Jeavons *et al.* 1966).

Gastaut *et al.* (1962) did not find abnormal responses with rates above 40 f.sec. Abnormalities in responses to single flash have been reported by Bickford *et al.* (1953), Jeavons (1966), Kooi (1971). Walter *et al.* (1946), Turton (1952) and Melsen

(1959) used an electronic trigger circuit whereby the photostimulator could be triggered by the patient's own EEG. Gastaut and Corriol (1951), and Haneke (1963) and Capron (1966) used double flashes, but this technique has been used only rarely in relation to photosensitivity. Some authors use sweeps of increasing and decreasing rates of flash. Doose *et al.* (1969a) used an increasing frequency from 4 f.sec. to 20 f. sec. over a period of 30 seconds, and then a decrease from 20 to 4 f.sec. also over 30 seconds. Others, like Carterette and Symmes (1952) and Troupin (1966), use only one flash rate at a time.

## Duration of IPS

The variation in duration is as great as the variation in the methods of using different frequencies, and often no details are given. The periods of continuous exposure to IPS vary from 2 seconds (Rao and Prichard 1955, Jeavons *et al.* 1966) to 20 minutes (Herrlin 1954).

A few authors gave a fixed period of flicker followed by a fixed interval— Carterette and Symmes (1952) used 10 seconds flashing with 10 seconds interval, Kooi *et al.* (1960) gave 20 seconds, and Johnson (1963) gave 30 seconds exposure to flicker at intervals of 30 seconds. Johnson noted that 22 of 110 helicopter pilots showed some theta activity during photic stimulation and appeared to be drowsy.

Brausch and Ferguson (1965) found that successive EEG responses to the same stimulus tended to diminish if the stimuli were a few seconds apart and their trials were therefore spaced at intervals of at least 30 seconds. On the other hand Walter and Walter (1949) found that the latency of the seizure response tended to diminish at each exposure, and after 6 or 7 trials spikes and jerks appeared after only a second or so of stimulation. Capron (1966) reported both habituation and summation of responses and Hishikawa *et al.* (1967) reported some potentiation of responses following the provocation of seizure discharges, and some variation from day to day. Bickford and Klass (1969) found that responses to IPS varied even when the external conditions, including the parameters of the photic stimulus, were kept apparently constant. However, the patient described by Bickford and Klass was stimulated with her eyes *closed* and therefore the position of the eyeball was not controlled. Chatrian *et al.* (1970) found the latency and duration of the abnormal response varied from one stimulation to the next, whether the stimulus was pattern or flickering light. It should also be noted that most authors have not attempted to control the internal milieu.

There is little doubt that the longer the period of continuous exposure to flickering light the greater the risk of inducing a fit. It is also of interest that the highest incidence of 'abnormality' evoked by IPS in normal children is in the series described by Brandt *et al.* (1961), who gave 6 minutes' continuous exposure to IPS.

## Intensity

Adrian and Matthews (1934) originally reported that photic driving depended in part on the intensity of the flickering light. Marshall *et al.* (1953) commented that the threshold for production of abnormal responses depended on the intensity but gave no figures, apart from mentioning that the intensity had to be doubled if monocular stimulation was used (see page 18). Pantelakis *et al.* (1962) reduced the intensity of the

13

light by 11 per cent, 15 per cent and 35 per cent by using one, two or three sheets of paper in front of the lamp. However, since the glass of their stroboscope was plain, this alteration diffused the light as well as changing the intensity.

It is almost impossible to compare the intensity used by one worker with that used by anyone else, since the definitions show such variation. The following examples illustrate the difficulty: 300,000 foot candles (Bickford *et al.* 1953), 200,000 f.c. (Carterette and Symmes 1952), 80,000 f.c. (Herrlin 1954), 10,000 to 333,000 according to the setting of the photostimulator and the flash rate (Melsen 1959), 0.45 Joule with peak intensity 150.104 at 20 cm. (Hishikawa *et al.* 1967), 100,000 candle power at 25 f.sec. (Pantelakis *et al.* 1962), Knott intensity 11 (Doose *et al.* 1969a). Many authors give no information. Brausch and Ferguson (1965) gave most information about intensity, and found that abnormal responses to IPS depended in part on the intensity of the light source. They compared different colours of flash with respect to 'the luminance flux per unit area incident at the cornea ('illuminance')'. They defined luminance as 'the intensity per unit area at the source' and gave details of their mathematical methods.

### Distance of lamp

The distance of the light source from the patient's eyes has varied from 2.5 cm. (Wadlington and Riley 1965) to 115 cm. (Pallis and Louis 1961). A distance of less than 10 cm. has been used by four authors (Walter and Walter 1949, Carterette and Symmes 1952, Kooi *et al.* 1960, Wadlington and Riley 1965). Most authors placed the lamp between 10 and 30 cm, a distance of between 10 and 20 cm. being used by Herrlin (1954), Melsen (1959), Kooi *et al.* (1960), Capron (1966), Hishikawa *et al.* (1967) and Doose *et al.* (1969a), whilst Laget and Humbert (1954), Pantelakis *et al.* (1962) and Brausch and Ferguson used 25 or 30 cm. Bickford *et al.* (1952), Rao and Prichard (1955), Pallis and Louis (1961) and Forster and Campos (1964) used distances greater than 30 cm, the latter authors using 1 metre during conditioning therapy.

### Background illumination

Although it is clear that the effectiveness of photic stimulation is related to the intensity of the light source, this relationship is dependent not on the absolute intensity, but on the intensity of the light source *relative* to the background illumination. Many authors do not comment on the background illumination, but some have noted variation in effectiveness under differing conditions of background illumination, or have systematically varied the intensity of an illuminated background.

Pallis and Louis (1961) commented that when photic stimulation was given in a darkened room photoconvulsive responses and their clinical concomitants were more easily evoked. To produce similar abnormalities when photic stimulation was used against a bright background, much longer exposure to the stimulation was necessary. Forster *et al.* (1964) noted that raising the background level of illumination would in fact abolish the provocative nature of the photostimulator and indeed used this technique as one of their methods of extinction therapy. Harding *et al.* (1969)

14

confirmed this finding and used control of relative intensity in their therapeutic device (see page 99).

**Diffusion**

When a diffusion screen is placed between the photostimulator and the patient a uniform unpatterned stimulus is presented. Walter and Walter (1949) found increased abnormality on photic stimulation given with diffused light, and this finding has been confirmed by Davidson and Watson (1956) and Brausch and Ferguson (1965). Similar findings were observed by Pantelakis *et al.* (1962) and Troupin (1966), who reported that the effect of using a diffusion screen was similar to the effect of the eyes-closed condition, and suggested that the eyelids may act as a diffuser.

**Pattern**

Bickford *et al.* (1953) reported EEG abnormalities induced by looking at patterned clothing. Bickford and Klass (1962) reported on 10 cases who showed EEG abnormalities during photic stimulation; during pattern presentation they found that pattern was most effective when it was simple, fine, and geometric, with sharp contrast. Movement of the pattern increased its effectiveness. In a later report (1969) these authors suggested that the orientation of the pattern was important, vertical lines being more effective than angled lines. Evidence of pattern sensitivity was found in 5 per cent of patients sensitive to photic stimulation.

Chatrian *et al.* (1970) carried out an extensive study of four patients, and reported similar findings to those of Bickford and Klass (1969). In addition they found that the pattern was most effective when it impinged on the macula and that the photoconvulsive range was increased when the pattern was illuminated by photic stimulation. Another pattern found to be effective was the 'quadrilled' or grid pattern. Jeavons *et al.* (1972a) found this pattern to be more effective than any other, although it should be noted that the pattern was superimposed on the photostimulator, that is, the flickering light shone through the pattern. These authors noted a marked increase in the ease with which photoconvulsive responses were elicited without increase of intensity (see page 77). Engel (1974) used a less effective chequer-board pattern instead of a fine grid pattern (see page 81).

**Colour**

The first report on the effect of red flickering light was made by Walter and Walter (1949), and the effects of photic stimulation with red, green or blue lights have been described subsequently by many investigators, usually using Wratten filters in front of the lamp of the photostimulator. Particular studies have been made by Carterette and Symmes (1952), Pantelakis *et al.* (1962), Brausch and Ferguson (1965), Troupin (1966), and Capron (1966). Increased sensitivity to red light has been reported by Livingston (1952), Carterette and Symmes (1952), Marshall *et al.* (1953), Pantelakis *et al.* (1962), Brausch and Ferguson (1965) and Capron (1966), the latter author finding that 41 of her 66 patients were more sensitive to red light on at least one occasion, and that sensitivity to red light was greater in those with grand mal or myoclonic epilepsy than those with petit mal or other types of fit. On the other hand

Bickford and Klass (1962) found little difference with different coloured lights and Rao and Prichard (1955) and Troupin (1966) reported variable results. Bickford *et al.* (1953) found only very slight evidence of increased sensitivity to red light and pointed out how difficult it was to assess the influence of red light because of the filtering effect of the eyelids and the fact that sensitivity to flicker was greater when the eyes were closed. Pantelakis *et al.* (1962) felt that the increased sensitivity to red light was more apparent than real and was due to the eyelids acting as a red filter, thus reducing the effect of blue and green flicker. However, Brausch and Ferguson (1965) also considered the action of the eyelids as a red filter and did not regard the lowering of the threshold to flickering light as entirely explained by this theory. They felt that the eyelids may act as a diffuser and that a greater area of retina may therefore be illuminated. Capron showed that a red filter in front of the lamp caused little reduction of the ERG when the eyes were closed, whereas blue, green and neutral reduced it considerably. Putting a red filter in front of open eyes did not increase EEG discharges.

Bickford and Klass (1962) used a combination of coloured lights and patterns and elicited spike and wave responses in the EEG while the patient looked at the television screen. Bickford and Klass (1969) commented on the lack of adequate controls in investigations of the effect of colour.

A number of authors have reported clinical relief of seizures following the use of tinted, polarised or filtered glass spectacles, particularly if the glass is chosen on the basis of the patient's response to photic stimulation with coloured lights (see page 83).

**The state of the patient's eyes during IPS**

Some authors give no information as to whether the patient's eyes were open or closed during IPS. Some authors tested the effect of IPS only while the patient's eyes were closed, others only when they were open. In addition, it is not always clear whether the patient's eyes were initially open and were then closed during IPS or whether the stimulation was given with the eyes already closed (see below).

The majority of authors found that abnormalities were more likely to be evoked when the patients' eyes were closed (Bickford *et al.* 1953, Brazier 1953, Melsen 1959, Pallis and Louis 1961, Pantelakis *et al.* 1962, Brausch and Ferguson 1965, Troupin 1966, Bickford and Klass 1969, Kooi 1971), and a number of theories were propounded to explain this. Two suggestions were (1) that the eyelids acted as a red filter (see page 84), although Troupin (1966) found less activation on testing with eyes open using a red filter than on testing with eyes closed, and (2) Brausch and Ferguson's (1965) theory that the eyelids diffused light, thus increasing the area of retina which was illuminated. Davidson and Watson (1956) and Bickford and Klass (1969) supported the diffusion theory, the latter suggesting that reduction in visual pattern input also played a part. Loss of visual attention was suggested as a factor by Pantelakis *et al.* (1962).

Very few authors found more abnormalities when the eyes were open during IPS (Mawdsley 1961, Jeavons *et al.* 1966). Carterette and Symmes (1952), who were mainly interested in the effect of colour, tested their patients only in the eyes-open state.

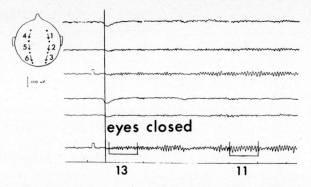

**Fig. 2.** 'Squeak' activity. The alpha rhythm is faster (13 c.sec.) immediately following eye closure than it is when the eyes have been closed for 4-5 seconds (11 c.sec.) (from Jeavons 1969).

However, many authors made no distinction between the *state* of 'eyes closed' and the *act* of 'eye closure', despite all the evidence that during the one or two seconds immediately following eye closure the state of cerebral activity may be very different from that at any other time. For example, the frequency of alpha rhythm is often faster by 2 c.sec. at this time (fig. 2), a phenomenon known as 'squeak' (Storm van Leeuwen and Bekkering 1958). In addition a number of patients show spontaneous spike and wave discharges immediately following eye closure (Bickford *et al.* 1953, Atzev 1962, Green 1966, 1968, Jeavons 1966, Kooi 1971). Atzev (1962) found this type of abnormality in 29 of 1000 patients with epilepsy, and Jeavons (1966) reported spontaneous spike and wave discharges following eye closure in 7 per cent of 402 patients who had EEG abnormalities evoked by IPS. An increase in abnormality evoked by IPS immediately after eye closure has been reported by Walter and Walter (1949), Lloyd-Smith and Henderson (1951), and Brausch and Ferguson (1965).

It is therefore possible that the apparent increased sensitivity with eyes closed was due to the effect of closing the eyes. This explanation almost certainly applies to the findings of Pantelakis *et al.* (1962), since their method of IPS involved the patient closing the eyes during the period of flicker and the subsequent responses were classified as being 'eyes-closed' ones. A method in common use in EEG departments in the United Kingdom is to ask the patient to close his eyes immediately the flicker starts.

The importance of distinguishing the states of 'eyes open' and 'eyes closed' from the act of 'eye closure' was first suggested by Harding (personal communication, 1962) and has been stressed by Jeavons *et al.* (1966, 1972*b* and Jeavons 1969).

Brazier (1953) discussed the effect of *opening* the eyes, pointing out that spike and wave discharges which were evoked by IPS with eyes closed were sometimes inhibited on opening the eyes, and that responses evoked by single flashes disappeared on opening the eyes. Bickford *et al.* (1953) described spike and wave discharges evoked by a startling stimulus such as a hand clap or single flash of light, and one wonders if this stimulus evoked a blink, so that the discharge was really evoked by sudden eye closure. Blinking is known to evoke spike and wave (Green 1966), and also to induce fits in some cases (Robertson 1954, Andermann *et al.* 1962, Gastaut and Tassinari 1966, Green 1966).

## Monocular stimulation

The effect of monocular stimulation has been reported by a number of authors, the first being Bickford *et al.* (1952), who found that the photomyoclonic response was inhibited, although the photoconvulsive response could still be obtained, when stimulation was applied to one eye only. Marshall *et al.* (1953) found that the intensity of the light had to be doubled during monocular stimulation in order to reach the convulsive threshold. Robertson (1954) found that EEG abnormalities induced by IPS were reduced or absent if one eye was occluded. Reduction of abnormality on monocular stimulation was confirmed by Davidson and Watson (1956), Brausch and Ferguson (1965), Green (1966), Jeavons *et al.* (1966), Hishikawa *et al.* (1967). Forster and Campos (1964) and Forster *et al.* (1965) used monocular stimulation with success as a method of extinction therapy, but Braham (1967) and Harding *et al.* (1969) did not find this method useful. Green (1966) used an eye-patch for therapy, and Jeavons and Harding (1970) suggested covering the eye with the palm of the hand as a therapeutic method in 'television epilepsy'. Chatrian *et al.* (1970) found reduction of abnormality induced by monocular pattern stimulation in pattern-sensitive epileptic patients, and postulated that the reduction was due to a decreased input to the visual cortex.

Parsons-Smith (1953) reported the effect of monocular stimulation, using an opaque black eye patch, in patients with amblyopia due to strabismus. Photic driving was recorded in both occipital regions whichever eye was stimulated, but suppression of alpha rhythm sometimes did not occur when the amblyopic eye was stimulated. In three patients with epilepsy spike and wave discharges were evoked only when the sound eye was stimulated (see page 75).

## Other factors

Rodin *et al.* (1955) found that less abnormality was evoked by IPS during sleep and Hishikawa *et al.* (1967) did not evoke spike and wave discharges during light or deep sleep, but found that during REM sleep the discharges were the same as occurred during waking. However, Meier-Ewert and Broughton (1967) found that photoconvulsive responses were even more decreased in the REM stage of sleep than in the non-REM stages. Rabending *et al.* (1967) reported the influence of photic stimulation on the heart rate in photosensitive epileptic patients and compared the responses to those in normal controls, finding that both groups showed tachycardia and bradycardia.

# CHAPTER 3

# EEG Studies

## Abnormal responses to IPS

In nearly all cases of photosensitive epilepsy, and particularly in 'television' epilepsy, photosensitivity has been proven by the finding of abnormal responses to IPS during electroencephalography. Livingston (1952), Klapatek (1959) and Charlton and Hoefer (1964) reported cases in whom there was no abnormality on IPS.

Although there is general agreement that the most common type of abnormality evoked by IPS in the photosensitive epileptic patient is a bilateral spike and wave discharge with a slow wave component at 2.5-3.5 c.sec., or a polyspike and wave discharge, it is sometimes difficult to evaluate the EEG findings in the literature because a number of authors do not define or describe in detail the abnormalities evoked by IPS, and many do not give illustrations. It is also rare for information to be given about the patient's basic record (i.e. that taken at rest and during hyperventilation).

Bickford *et al.* (1952) clearly differentiated two types of abnormal response to IPS—the photomyoclonic and photoconvulsive responses. The *photomyoclonic response* is seen in the anterior regions only and consists of anterior spikes in the EEG at the same rate as the flash, with clinical accompaniment of jerking movements of the muscles round the eyes. This response is seen with the eyes closed and disappears on eye opening. The *photoconvulsive response* (PCR) is an abnormal EEG discharge seen in all areas, the discharge usually consisting of spike and wave or atypical spike and wave. It occurs with eyes open or closed, and the clinical accompaniment may be turning of the eyes or an arrest of speech (i.e. an absence). Photoconvulsive responses may be seen at all ages whereas photomyoclonic discharges are commonest in adults.

Capron (1966) described seven types of abnormal response to IPS:

1. spikes and spike and wave with or without an associated absence, or polyspike and wave
2. clinical fits—absence or grand mal
3. degraded spike and wave
4. disorganised theta rhythms with spikes, in the occipital regions
5. occipital slow rhythms on eye closure
6. recruitment of occipital rhythms at 7-9 c.sec. spreading to the Rolandic and frontal regions with some myoclonic jerking
7. photomyoclonic responses

Gangelberger and Cvetko (1956) also divided the responses to IPS according to the EEG abnormalities and the clinical fits which were evoked by the flicker.

Jeavons (1969) divided the responses evoked by photic stimulation into three groups according to whether the responses were confined to the anterior regions (photomyoclonic), were confined to the posterior regions (photic driving, responses to single flashes, and occipital spikes), or were widespread, bilateral and involved both anterior and posterior regions (photoconvulsive). These responses are described later (see page 57).

### Photomyoclonic responses

Gastaut (1950) described a 'myoclonic' response characterized by pre-central and frontal spikes which were bilateral, synchronous and at the same frequency as the flash. They occurred with eyes closed and were associated with jerking of the muscles. The spikes showed a progressive increase in amplitude ('recruitment'). Bickford *et al.* (1952) called this response 'photomyoclonic' and regarded it as a normal response to high-intensity light stimulation, finding it in half of their normal subjects. Gastaut *et al.* (1958) found the photomyoclonic response could be evoked in 0.3 per cent of normal subjects, in 3 per cent of patients with epilepsy, in 13 per cent of patients with brain stem lesions and in 17 per cent of psychiatric patients. Shagass (1954) found a photomyoclonic response in 20 per cent of psychiatric patients but neither he, nor Gastaut *et al.* (1958) nor Kooi *et al.* (1960) found the response assisted in differential diagnosis.

Bickford (1966) described 'microreflexes' evoked by IPS, and Meier-Ewert and Broughton (1967) regarded photomyoclonic responses as an enhancement of these subclinical physiological reflexes. These authors found that photomyoclonic responses were diminished in NREM sleep and on arousal from NREM sleep and during REM sleep.

### Photoconvulsive responses

Photoconvulsive responses are discharges evoked by IPS which are bilateral and recorded simultaneously from all areas of the scalp. The commonest form of PCR is a spike and wave discharge with a slow wave component at 3-3.5 c.sec. Typical 3 c.sec. spike and wave discharges with an associated 'absence' have been reported by many authors.

Ebe *et al.* (1969) found that intravenous diazepam inhibited photoconvulsive responses. Meier-Ewert and Broughton (1967), who studied a somewhat special group of patients with epilepsy (including two patients with Unverricht-Lundborg syndrome and one with progressing dyssnergia cerebellaris myoclonica and grand mal), found that PCRs were diminished during NREM sleep, and even further diminished in REM sleep. On arousal from NREM sleep, long episodes of myoclonus occurred and PCRs could not be elicited. On arousal from REM sleep, myoclonus did not occur and PCR could be elicited. The myoclonic jerking on arousal was commoner in the 'petit mal' patients than among the Unverricht-Lundborg patients. These authors distinguished these myoclonic episodes from those which occurred as transient isolated jerks on waking mainly on the basis of their more or less continuous nature. The jerks never terminated in a grand mal and tended to decrease in intensity rather than increase.

### Sensitivity limits

Pantelakis *et al.* (1962) tested each patient over a range of frequencies, using one frequency at a time, and starting with slower frequencies and gradually using faster flash rates. They compared the range of frequencies evoking abnormality with eyes open to the range with eyes closed, but they did not compare individual patients according to their sensitivity ranges. Jeavons *et al.* (1966) established upper and lower sensitivity limits and ranges and related these to a number of other factors.

## Fits induced by IPS

The commonest type of PCR is a spike and wave discharge which may be brief or may be associated with a typical petit mal absence. Such an absence may be triggered by the IPS and continue after the flicker stimulus has stopped. Lloyd Smith and Henderson (1951) described how IPS could induce myoclonic jerking which might progress to a generalized seizure, and Daly and Bickford (1951) reported major seizures induced by IPS. A number of authors describe the occurrence of generalized tonic-clonic seizures during IPS. In most cases this unhappy result of photic stimulation appears to be due to three factors, alone or in combination: a long period of stimulation (Herrlin 1954), the use of a trigger or double flash (Melsen 1959, Haneke 1963), and the continuation of photic stimulation after the appearance of EEG abnormality (Daly and Bickford 1951, Haneke 1963, Wadlington and Riley 1965). Capron (1966), who used a relatively short (15-20 second) period of stimulation, commented that grand mal seizures were rare but occurred after IPS had stopped, and that there was usually no EEG warning though there might be a 'flattening of alpha rhythm'. Pantelakis *et al.* (1962) and Hishikawa *et al.* (1967) used short periods of IPS stopping the stimulus as soon as any abnormality was evoked. These authors only evoked myoclonic jerks.

Jeavons (1966, 1969) reported myoclonic jerking in 29 per cent of 402 patients who showed abnormality on IPS. Two-thirds of the patients who jerked suffered from epilepsy.

Other types of fit induced by IPS are rare. Adversive fits have been reported by Bickford *et al.* (1953), Daly *et al.* (1959) and Brausch and Ferguson (1965), and psychomotor fits by Melsen (1959).

Apart from the occurrence of epileptic fits, peculiar sensations may be experienced. Adrian and Matthews (1934) reported them in normal adults, and Petersen *et al.* (1968) found that some children experienced sensations, though these authors said that the sensations were not associated with EEG abnormality. Brausch and Ferguson (1965) also reported subjective sensations occurring in patients.

It is extremely difficult to evaluate the literature because abnormalities are often not defined or illustrated and techniques vary. Mundy Castle (1953) reported that 3.9 per cent of young normal adults showed an abnormal response to IPS, but he included both photomyoclonic and photoconvulsive responses. Herrlin (1954) found paroxysmal responses in 1.4 per cent of 70 normal children. Ulett and Johnson (1958) found 'paroxysmal activation' in 4.4 per cent of a group of young normal adults, while Gastaut *et al.* (1958) found no spike and wave discharges in 500 normal subjects. Kooi *et al.* (1960) found photoconvulsive responses in 3 of 90 normal subjects. Brandt *et al.* (1961) found 'paroxysmal EEG responses' in 26 per cent of normal children, with generalized spike and wave discharges occurring in 14 per cent. This high incidence is unique and is attributable to these authors' technique of giving photic stimulation for as long as six minutes.

Petersen *et al.* (1968) found 'paroxysmal abnormality' in 5 per cent of a normal population of 757 children, but 3 c.sec. spike and wave discharges were seen in only 7 children, that is, less than 1 per cent. Under the heading of 'paroxysmal abnormality' they included bi-occipital responses of slow waves and initial spike (most probably an exaggerated VEP) and focal sharp wave or spike. They used a Kaiser photostimulator at 0.2 joule intensity, and this photostimulator is very potent because of the metal grid (see page 77). Furthermore stimulation was continued for a long period and the method was a little unusual, being as follows:

40 seconds each of 7 flash rates = 280 seconds,
20 seconds each of 12 flash rates = 240 seconds,
2 flash rates for 3 seconds each 10 times = 60 seconds,
1 flash rate for 5 seconds 6 times = 30 seconds,
Total time exposed to flashing light = 610 seconds.

With a period of 10 minutes' exposure to photic stimulation it is not surprising that some abnormalities were evoked. Unfortunately it is a little difficult to assess this paper because the distance from the lamp is not given, nor is there any mention of whether the eyes were open or closed. However, if, despite a strongly provocative method, spike and wave discharges were evoked in only 1 per cent, with normal techniques it is unlikely that spike and wave discharges will be found in normal subjects, provided they do not have photosensitive siblings.

**The clinical significance of photoconvulsive responses**

It is clear from the above that photoconvulsive responses which consist of spike and wave discharges at 3 c.sec. are very rare in normal subjects.

The incidence of abnormal responses in clinical populations varies considerably, doubtless owing to the variations in definitions of abnormality and the techniques used. Herrlin (1954) found abnormality in 25 per cent of 362 children with epilepsy, abnormalities being particularly common in those aged 10-15 years. Gastaut *et al.* (1958) found spike and wave discharges on IPS in 15 per cent of all epileptic patients, and in 25 per cent of patients with 'centrencephalic' epilepsy. The incidence of abnormalities induced by IPS was much greater in the generalised epilepsies than in other types. Spike and wave discharges were found in less than 5 per cent of patients with non-epileptic conditions. These authors regarded spike and wave discharges evoked by IPS as almost specific for centrencephalic epilepsy. Kooi *et al.* (1960) also found that photoconvulsive responses were suggestive of a convulsive tendency. Melsen (1959) found spike and wave discharges in 27 of 1366 patients and in 26 of these the diagnosis was cryptogenic epilepsy.

Jeavons (1966) found spike and wave responses in 2.8 per cent of 14,141 patients referred for EEG investigation—a figure similar to that of Gastaut *et al.* (1958). Spike and wave discharges evoked by IPS were very significantly related to a history of epilepsy (Jeavons 1969), and polyspike and wave discharges were seen only in patients with a definite diagnosis of epilepsy. All patients in whom an absence with spike and wave activity was induced by IPS had a definite clinical history of epilepsy. A photoconvulsive response did not necessarily indicate that the patient had photosensitive epilepsy, nor was the type of PCR related to the type of clinical fit. However, myoclonic jerking evoked by IPS was associated with a definite history of epilepsy in 67 per cent of cases, with a history of suspected epilepsy in 19 per cent, and with a non-epileptic condition in 14 per cent. One can conclude that myoclonic jerking evoked by IPS is a strong pointer to a clinical diagnosis of epilepsy.

Spike and wave discharges in which the slow wave component is between 4 and 7 c.sec. (theta spike and wave) appear to be less common in patients with epilepsy and more common in those with a non-epileptic, or doubtfully epileptic condition (Melsen 1959, Kooi *et al.* 1960, Jeavons 1966). Scollo-Lavizzari (1971) reported a 5-7 year follow-up of 142 non-epileptic patients who initially showed 'epileptiform' discharges in their EEGs during IPS. Only 1.4 per cent developed seizures and only 37 per cent of the remainder still showed the 'epileptiform' discharges after 6 years.

## Basic EEG

Comparatively few authors give information about the basic EEG records of their photosensitive patients and differentiate those with normal basic EEGs from those with spontaneous spike and wave activity.

Jeavons *et al.* (1966) reported a difference between those patients whose EEGs showed spontaneous spike and wave discharges and those whose basic EEG was normal and who only showed spike and wave discharges when exposed to flickering light.

Lloyd Smith and Henderson (1951) found that 13 of their 40 patients showed spike and wave discharges *only* during IPS. On the other hand Bickford *et al.* (1953) stated that three-quarters of their patients had spontaneous spike and wave discharges. Herrlin (1954) did not separate 3 c.sec. spike and wave from other types of abnormality induced by IPS, merely classifying responses to IPS as pathological or not pathological, but he did report that some patients had a normal basic EEG. Melsen (1959) found abnormality on IPS in 150 (11.2 per cent) of 735 patients whose basic EEGs did not show 'paroxysmal abnormality'. Hughes (1960) reported spike and wave discharges in 42 cases of whom 10 showed abnormality *only* on IPS. Capron (1966) found 14 per cent of 161 EEGs were normal apart from on IPS. Of these 161, 88 showed 'alterations majeures', by which was meant spike and wave. However, degraded spike and wave discharges were rated as 'alterations mineures' which makes it somewhat difficult to evaluate the findings, since a number of other authors appear to group together spike and wave and degraded spike and wave.

## Spontaneous abnormality on eye closure

A number of patients show spontaneous spike and wave discharges in the EEG immediately after closing their eyes. Cases have been reported by Bickford *et al.* (1953), Atzev (1962) and Jeavons (1966), among others (see page 17). Jeavons (1969) stated that spike and wave discharges which occurred in the basic EEG record immediately after eye closure almost always indicated that abnormality would be evoked by IPS.

Green (1966) reported spike and wave discharges occurring on blinking and on eye closure, and found that these discharges did not occur in total darkness or on passive eye closure. In 1968 the same author reported that EEG abnormalities could

23

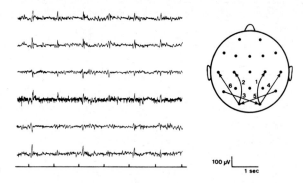

**Fig. 3.** Type of evoked potential that can sometimes be seen in EEG recordings of normal subjects from electrodes over the visual cortex. The bottom trace shows the occurrence of each light flash. (From Harding 1974.)

be induced by eye closure in the dark, but passive eye closure was not effective. Rossi *et al.* (1969) reported the case of a boy whose myoclonic absences were evoked by eye closure and in whom EEG abnormality occurred on active and passive closing of the eyes, but not in the dark. Jeavons *et al.* (1972b) found that abnormality did not occur after eye closure in total darkness.

Although one of the 4 cases described by Green (1968) was typical in showing a spike and wave discharge immediately following eye closure and PCR during photic stimulation, the other 3 cases showed unusual features. In one, eye closure was followed by continuous polyspike and wave discharges and myoclonic jerking of the eyelids until the eyes were opened. There was no evidence that flickering light had precipitated fits in everyday life. The response occurred, but to a lesser extent, in the dark. One wonders whether this prolonged and very unusual response was a conditioned one, rather than being a photosensitive one. In the second case the response increased with increased pressure or squeezing tight of the eyelids; it occurred in the dark, and no abnormality was induced by IPS. The third patient did not have fits, nor was there any spike and wave activity on eye closure, the abnormality being sharp waves.

## Visual Evoked Potentials (VEP)

EEG responses to visual stimuli were first observed by Adrian and Matthews (1934). They showed that regularly repeated flashes of light could elicit a 'following' response in the EEG recorded from the visual cortex. A small percentage of the population show a supra-normal response to single flashes (fig. 3), but a similar response might be hidden in the EEG of other individuals. Although the EEG is a real and meaningful signal it is relatively unrelated to incoming sensory stimuli. However, somewhere in the 'noise' of this spontaneous signal is hidden the tiny electrical response to each specific stimulus. Obviously if these responses are to be studied a technique is needed which highlights the response or reduces the spontaneous EEG activity.

24

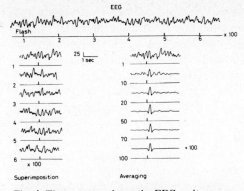

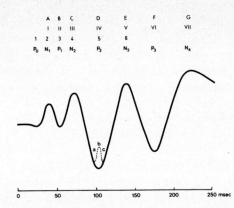

**Fig. 4.** The top trace shows the EEG as it occurs at the time of a sequence of flashes. The left hand column shows the same EEG divided into periods corresponding to each flash. By superimposing these traces (or looking down the column) it is possible to see a common negative wave occurring approximately 250 m.sec. after the flash. The right hand column shows the effect of averaging or summation, and it can be seen that the background activity slowly decays since it is random in relation to the flash and the sample period, whereas the evoked potential—which is time-locked to the flash—becomes proportionately more clear. (From Harding 1974.)

**Fig. 5.** Idealised visual evoked potential giving the notation of the components according to various authors.
First row, Dustman and Beck 1969; second row, Ciganek 1961; third row, Gastaut and Regis 1964 (transposed to Arabic from Roman numerals); fourth row, Harding 1974. At 100 m.sec. the a, b, and c components are those described by Gastaut and Regis as *Va, Vb, Vc*. (From Harding 1974.)

Dawson (1951, 1954) first applied the 'averaging' or summation technique to EEGs. This technique operates on the assumption that the 'evoked' response will be time-locked to the stimulus while the background noise of the spontaneous EEG will be random in its relation to the stimulus. When a stimulus is repetitively presented and the EEG on each occasion is stored, any common features or 'evoked responses' will add together to produce a clearer averaged evoked potential (fig. 4).

*VEP in normals*

The visual evoked potential is usually displayed as a plot of amplitude against time. Its shape depends partially on the stimulus used and partially on the state of the subject. If a transient flash stimulus (as provided by a photostimulator) is presented at a repetition rate of less than 3/second, its format is similar to that of Figure 5. Although most authors agree on the evoked potential components observed, the nomenclature given to the components varies widely (Harding 1974).

*VEP in epilepsy*

Although Dawson (1951, 1954) devised the averaging computer to overcome the difficulty of extracting somatosensory evoked potentials from background noise in patients with myoclonic epilepsy, relatively few studies of visual evoked potentials have been made in epilepsy. Cernácek and Cigánek (1962) noted a decrease in amplitude of the early components of the VEP and an increase in wave V in patients suffering from epilepsy, compared to a normal group. Gastaut *et al.* (1963) and Lucking *et al.* (1970) reported an overall reduction in amplitude of the visual evoked potential. Bergamini and Bergamasco (1967) and Needham *et al.* (1971) report an increase in amplitude of late components and after-discharge of the VEP in centrencephalic epilepsy, whereas Jonkman (1967) found no clear differences between patients with grand mal epilepsy and a normal population. Ebe *et al.* (1963) and Morocutti *et al.* (1964) found an increase in amplitude and a reduction in latency of the VEP in patients with epilepsy.

*VEP in photosensitive epilepsy*

Gastaut and Regis (1964) first noted enhancement of the amplitude of certain components of the VEP in patients with photosensitive epilepsy. In these patients they observed that wave 5 (positive at 140 m.sec.) was increased and that in particular the $5_b$ component was increased until it exceeded the amplitude of all other components. When the patients' seizures decreased either spontaneously or with drug treatment, the $5_b$ component also disappeared. Bergamini and Bergamasco (1967) reported that in patients with myoclonic epilepsy, the waves $5_a$ and $5_b$ of Gastaut and Regis were increased in amplitude particularly during seizures induced by photic stimulation. Similar findings were reported by Broughton *et al.* (1969), who also found an increase in latency of the $5_b$ component. Green (1969) found enhancement of the $5_a$ and $5_c$ components.

Brezny (1965), Morocutti *et al.* (1966), Creutzfeldt *et al.* (1966), Bablouzion *et al.* (1969) and Lucking *et al.* (1970) all found a general increase in amplitude of the VEP, but with the exception of Bablouzion *et al.* and Lucking *et al.* the same findings were observed in all types of epilepsy.

Hishikawa *et al.* (1967) observed in their photosensitive patients that negative occipital spikes were induced by single, double or trains of flashes (IPS). They concluded that the occipital spikes were enhanced components of the VEP occurring at a latency of 45 m.sec. (three cases) and 88 m.sec. (three cases). These waves correspond respectively to wave 2 and 4 of Gastaut and Regis (1964). Panayiotopoulos *et al.* (1970, 1972) observed negative occipital spikes with a latency of 106 m.sec. corresponding to wave $P_2$ (Gastaut and Regis wave 5) of the VEP. In a further study in our laboratory, Dimitrakoudi *et al.* (1973) demonstrated that the occipital spike was an enhancement of Gastaut and Regis's wave $5_b$ (see page 91). Both Panayiotopoulos *et al.* and Dimitrakoudi *et al.* reported that the negative occipital spike appeared to act as a precursor of photoconvulsive responses.

CHAPTER 4

# Therapy

**Drugs**

There have been no large trials and no controlled trials of drugs in photosensitive epilepsy. Bickford *et al.* (1953) gave intravenous anticonvulsants to 7 patients and found that trimethadione, sodium amylobarbitone and phenacamide suppressed abnormality evoked by IPS. However, long-term clinical response did not parallel this short-term testing. Ganglberger and Cvetko (1956) also reported clinical response to trimethadione. Pantelakis *et al.* (1962) reported clinical improvement with pheno-barbitone. Rivano *et al.* (1968) reported that myoclonic seizures and EEG discharges induced by photic stimulation were inhibited by intravenous injections of nitrazepam. Ebe *et al.* (1969) found that intravenous diazepam inhibited photoconvulsive and photo-myoclonic responses in epileptic patients. The visual and somato-sensory evoked potentials were also modified. Livingston (1972) found no anticonvulsant particularly effective.

Doose and Gerken (1973) and Völzke and Doose (1973) suggested the use of sodium valproate (dipropylacetate) in photosensitivity, and preliminary trials by Jeavons and Clark (1974) and Jeavons and Maheshwari (1974) confirmed that this drug was effective in reducing spike and wave discharges evoked by IPS as well as those occurring spontaneously (see page 95).

**Conditioning**

The first attempt at applying conditioning techniques as a therapeutic procedure for photosensitive epilepsy was that of Forster and Campos (1964). Their patient had a history of photosensitive attacks and on investigation by EEG and photic stimulation was found to be sensitive to binocular stimulation, but was not sensitive when either eye was stimulated while the other eye was covered. Having satisfied themselves of the patient's response to binocular stimulation, they carried out a number of extinction trials in which the patient was exposed to intermittent photic stimulation to one eye only. After approximately six extinction trials, they found that the response to binocular stimulation had been markedly reduced and further extinction trials appeared to remove entirely the abnormal response to binocular stimulation. A similar method was used by Braham (1967), but failed to produce any extinction of the photosensitive response. Forster *et al.* (1964) again reported the monocular extinction method and followed this by two further methods of producing extinction of the photosensitive response. The second method consisted of establishing upper and lower limits of the frequency range of stimulation to which the patient was sensitive and administering a series of stimulations at a frequency just outside the sensitivity range. Following the trials the upper and lower limits of the sensitivity range were again investigated, and if no abnormal response occurred, repeated extinction trials were again administered closer to the limits of the sensitive range.

Forster and Campos found that this method was so difficult to use as to be impractical in a clinical situation.

The third method of extinction consisted of binocular stimulation with a photostimulator which was placed behind an opaque glass screen. Two photoflood bulbs in reflectors were placed on either side of the photostimulator. The brightness of the photofloods was controlled by a rheostat and was of such intensity that no clinical or EEG change occurred when the photostimulator was switched on. Repeated extinction trials were carried out with the intensity of the photofloods at a level which would block the response to the photostimulator, and then the light intensity of the photofloods was gradually reduced. This, of course, is a method of controlling the relative intensity of the photostimulator since it is known that the contrast between the flicker and background is important in the production of photosensitive responses. The authors found that this method was both the simplest and most successful of their three techniques. Harding *et al.* (1969a), however, reported failure of all three methods of extinction (see page 98).

### Spectacles

Since a reduction in the intensity of the flickering light has been found to reduce the photosensitive response, a number of authors have suggested the use of darkened, tinted or polaroid spectacles. Many authors have found that stimulation with red light causes a significant increase in photosensitivity (Walter and Walter 1949, Carterette and Symmes 1952, Marshall *et al.* 1953, Pantelakis *et al.* 1962, Brausch and Ferguson 1965, Capron 1966), and Carterette and Symmes (1952) proposed the use of glasses which eliminated the red end of the spectrum. This suggestion has been followed by other authors, including Bickford and Klass (1969). Although there is some anecdotal evidence for the benefit of using these glasses, it is very difficult to find any clear statistical evidence that they are successful. Harding *et al.* (1969a) reported on a more complicated form of spectacles incorporating a polaroid filter, a variable tint, and background illumination (see page 99ff).

### Monocular occlusion

Bickford *et al.* (1952) first reported the effect of monocular stimulation in photosensitivity. They found that although the photoconvulsive response could be elicited by monocular stimulation, the photomyoclonic response was totally inhibited. Marshall *et al.* (1953) found that in monocular stimulation the intensity of stimulation had to be doubled to provoke a photoconvulsive response (see page 18). This reduction of abnormality on monocular stimulation was confirmed by many authors including Green (1966) who suggested using an eye patch as a means of therapy. Jeavons and Harding (1970) confirmed the reduction on monocular stimulation and reported that covering one eye with the hand was an effective therapy (see page 96).

# Part II

# A Study of 460 Patients and 29 Relatives

# CHAPTER 5

# Clinical Studies

The 460 patients reported on in the remaining chapters of this book have been selected from those referred to the EEG Departments of Dudley Road Hospital and the Children's Hospital, Birmingham between 1961 and 1973 (see page 4). Not all the patients have been under our clinical care, but we have carried out EEG investigations on all of them. Clinical information is not always complete, for two main reasons. Firstly, the study is in part retrospective and the information in the earlier cases has been obtained from the original EEG request forms, the patients having been referred by many clinicians from many hospitals. It is only since 1966 that we have personally obtained histories from all patients. Secondly, it is not always possible to get accurate information about the precise nature of the fit or the circumstances in which it occurred, because an observer was not always present at the time of the fit. For example we may not know how near the patient was to the T.V. set, or whether the picture was faulty, or the nature of the programme.

In the past, when doctors were less aware of 'television epilepsy', the true diagnosis was sometimes not made until the EEG investigation had revealed abnormality during photic stimulation.

*Susan* (12 yrs.) was referred for EEG investigation because she had been found unconscious in her home when her parents returned after being out for the evening. Her younger brother, aged five, was in tears and unable to say what had happened. No diagnosis had been made, and the child showed no abnormality on physical examination. Her basic EEG was normal, but photic stimulation evoked spike and wave discharges. The parents were therefore asked about television viewing and it transpired that they had never previously left the children alone in the house and Susan had never before had to switch the T.V. set. She had had to switch off the set in order to persuade her brother to go to bed. She had then presumably had a fit which she could not remember and which her young brother could not describe.

The fact that a patient has had a fit whilst watching television does not necessarily mean that he or she is photosensitive. In Britain so many hours are spent watching television that it is inevitable that some patients will have a fit while sitting in front of a T.V. set. This is especially true as T.V. viewing is likely to occur in the evening and in itself is likely to induce drowsiness, and drowsiness is certainly a commoner precipitant of fits than flickering light. The diagnosis of photosensitive epilepsy has to be confirmed by the findings of EEG abnormality induced by photic stimulation.

### Clinical groups

Four hundred and fifty four patients had epilepsy, and they can be divided into those who have clinical fits induced by flickering light encountered in daily life, and those in whom abnormal discharges occur in the EEG during photic stimulation but

**TABLE II**

**Groups of patients according to clinical findings**

| Group | Fits with T.V. | Fits with light | Spontaneous fits | Total cases | |
|---|---|---|---|---|---|
| A | + | | | 160 | |
| B | + | | + | 99 | |
| C | + | + | | 21 | |
| D | + | + | + | 19 | |
| E | | + | + | 33 | |
| F | | | + | 122 | 454 |
| Non-epileptic | | | | 6 | |
| Relatives | | | | 29 | 489 |
| All T.V. (A + B + C + D) | | | | 299 | |
| Group I Flicker sensitive (A + C) | | | | 181 | |
| Group II Mixed (B + D + E) | | | | 151 | |
| Group III Spontaneous (F) | | | | 122 | |

in whom there is no evidence of clinical attacks being precipitated by flicker in everyday life. The patients can be further classified according to the nature of the precipitant and the presence or absence of 'spontaneous' fits.

We have therefore divided the patients into the following 6 groups (see Table II):

*Group A.* Fits have occurred *only* when watching T.V.

*Group B.* Fits have occurred while watching T.V. but also 'spontaneously' at times when there was no evidence of flickering light as a precipitant.

*Group C.* Fits have occurred while watching T.V. and also when the patient was exposed to flickering or bright light from other sources. No fit has occurred 'spontaneously'.

*Group D.* Fits have occurred with T.V., with flickering light from other sources, and also 'spontaneously'.

*Group E.* Fits have been evoked by flickering or bright light, but not by T.V. Spontaneous fits occur.

*Group F.* The patient has 'spontaneous' fits and there is no evidence of clinical photosensitivity. All patients in this group were selected because they showed spike and wave discharges in the EEG during photic stimulation.

Groups A, B, C and D, a total of 299 cases, all had fits induced by watching television. Groups A and C only had fits when exposed to flickering light, Groups B, D and E were photosensitive but also had 'spontaneous' fits, and Group F only had 'spontaneous' fits. Comparisons will be made later. Only 5 patients had a history of self-induced epilepsy (i.e., staring at a bright light source and waving their hands in front of their eyes), but 31 patients appeared to be impulsively or compulsively attracted to the T.V. screen. These 31 patients will be discussed later.

*Group A*

This is by far the largest group (160 cases), with 98 females and 62 males (ratio

158:100). The onset of fits is earlier in this group (mean 13.5 yrs.) than in the other photosensitive patients, though not as early as in those who are not light-sensitive (Group F). Nearly half these patients have normal basic EEGs and thus many of them do not require anticonvulsant therapy.

*Cynthia* (12 yrs.), the youngest of a family of four, usually watched T.V. from a distance of about four feet. One evening, when standing at the side of the set about two feet away from it, she turned to the right and then lost consciousness and had a tonic-clonic convulsion. When seen the following day she showed no abnormality on physical examination. There was no past history of any significance. She had not started menstruation, but was showing signs of puberty. Her basic EEG was normal, but photic stimulation evoked spike and wave discharges in response to flash rates between 7 and 68 per second. No anticonvulsants were given, but precautions for television viewing were adopted. She had no further fits and a year later her sensitivity range was 6-60 f.sec. with eyes open, and there was no abnormality with eyes closed.

*Patricia* (10 yrs.) was adjusting the T.V. set when she 'went blank', walked round the room 'like a robot', and then had a tonic-clonic attack followed by sleep for half an hour. A cousin, a boy aged 15, also had fits precipitated by television. The girl's basic EEG was abnormal, showing spike and wave and polyspike and wave discharges, often after eye closure. Photic stimulation evoked photoconvulsive responses with a range of 8-46 f.sec. with eyes open and 6-42 f.sec. with eyes closed. She was given phenobarbitone and remained free from further attacks.

*Jacqueline* (11 yrs.) was adjusting a faulty picture on the T.V. when she had a tonic-clonic fit with tongue biting. She was given phenobarbitone. Her basic EEG was normal and photic stimulation with eyes open induced spike and wave discharges over a range of 6-82 f.sec. No abnormality occurred with the eyes closed. Repeat EEG at 13 years showed a reduced range of sensitivity (12-28 f.sec.), but a different photostimulator was used. No further fit had occurred and the referring paediatrician was persuaded to reduce and stop the phenobarbitone. A third EEG taken at the age of 14 years, when the phenobarbitone had been stopped for more than a year, showed a sensitivity range of 7-42 f.sec. in response to the original photostimulator, the basic record remaining normal and no fits having occurred.

## Group B

This group is very similar to Group A and contains 99 patients, 61 being female and 38 male (ratio 160:100). The mean age of onset (13.7 yr.) is similar to Group A, as is the percentage with normal basic EEGs.

*Christine* (16 yrs.) approached the T.V. set to switch channels, but before she could touch the controls her left hand shook, her eyes rolled up and she had a tonic-clonic convulsion with incontinence and tongue biting. In addition she had myoclonic jerks for about an hour in the morning after walking, and during this time was unable to hold anything. Her basic EEG was abnormal, with spike and wave discharges occurring immediately after eye closure. Photic stimulation evoked spike and wave discharges with eyes open but none with eyes closed, the sensitivity range being 10-50 f.sec. Repeat EEG 6 months later showed a sensitivity range of 12-50 f.sec. She had remained free from fits despite continuing to adjust the controls of the T.V. set.

*Phillip* (13 yrs.) had a tonic-clonic fit induced by watching television, although his first fit had occurred in the cinema at the age of seven. He subsequently had a spontaneous fit in which he sustained severe facial burns. Later he became a ward orderly, and had a fit when adjusting the T.V. set on the ward. This fit was attributed to an electric shock from the set, but no fault was found by the hospital electricians. When he had a second tonic-clonic fit under similar circumstances he was referred for EEG examination. His basic record was normal but he showed spike and wave on photic stimulation with eyes open, with a range of 15-24 f.sec. He was already receiving anticonvulsants, and after taking the usual precautions for T.V. viewing he was free from fits until he was unexpectedly exposed to stroboscopes used by a 'pop' group.

*Mary J.* (26 yrs.) gave a history of being fascinated by the T.V. screen. She would find herself moving nearer and nearer to it whenever she entered the room and the set was on. She would start to jerk and would then have a tonic-clonic fit. She also had myoclonic jerks first thing in the morning, especially at the time of her periods. Her basic EEG was normal, and she showed spike and wave discharges with eyes open over a range of 12-36 f.sec. and with eyes closed over 28-32 f.sec. There was no abnormality with monocular stimulation. She was successfully treated with the use of an eye patch (see Chapter 8).

*Group C*

This is the smallest group, consisting of only 21 patients, 11 of whom are female and 10 male (ratio 110:100). The mean age is 20.6 years though the number of cases is too small for comparison with other groups. This group shows the lowest proportion of females. Like Group A, these patients do not have spontaneous fits.

*Robert* (8 yrs.) was sitting close to the T.V. set when he had a tonic-clonic fit. His father suffered from photosensitive epilepsy, but consistently refused to have an EEG. Robert's EEG showed spontaneous spike and wave discharges, but a constant photoconvulsive response was only evoked by photic stimulation at 10 f.sec. with eyes open. Single discharges were evoked by 16 and 18 f.sec., but not on repeat testing. Later he had a further tonic-clonic fit, also induced by television. He was fascinated by the T.V. screen and would be drawn nearer and nearer to it, so that a member of the family always had to be in the room to keep him away from the set. At times he was seen to flutter his eyelids in bright sunlight, and it is not clear whether he was voluntary blinking and thereby inducing spike and wave discharges and brief absences, or whether the eyelid flutter was the clinical manifestation of spike and wave activity. On several occasions, when standing on the side of the swimming baths he had brief disturbances of consciousness with clonic movements. These attacks were undoubtedly induced by sunlight reflected from the water. His EEG at the age of 9 years still showed spontaneous atypical spike and wave discharges, but on this occasion photic stimulation evoked spike and wave discharges at rates from 7 to 64 per second with eyes open and between 13 and 24 f.sec. with eyes closed. A further repeat a year later showed little change in the EEG, the sensitivity range being 7-70 f.sec.

*Jamil* had a tonic-clonic fit when he was 10 years old, while adjusting the T.V.

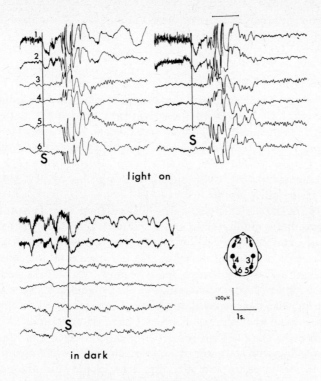

light on

in dark

**Fig. 6.** Effect of eye closure (S) in the light and in the
dark. In darkness there is no spike and wave discharge
evoked by eye closure. (From Panayiotopoulos 1974.)

set. Subsequently he had another major fit when travelling in a car along a tree-lined
road. He used to have a myoclonic jerk when the light in his bedroom was switched on
in the morning. On several occasions he was observed to be staring at the sun and
waving his hand across his eyes. Myoclonic jerks had occurred when he looked up
through the leaves of trees in bright sunlight. The garage doors at his home were
painted in alternate stripes of black and white and he had jerked when looking at
them in bright sunlight. When he was examined at the age of 16 years his basic EEG
was normal, but photic stimulation evoked spike and wave discharges and generalised
myoclonic jerking over a range of 38-50 f.sec. with eyes open, no abnormality
occurring with eyes closed.

*Lynne* (17 yrs.) was watching television at a friend's house when she had a
tonic-clonic fit with incontinence. She had a period three days later. The T.V. set was
brighter than the set she usually watched at home and the room was in semi-darkness.
She had experienced unpleasant sensations in a discotheque when flashing lights were
used. Her basic EEG was abnormal and showed occasional spikes in the occipital
regions, and spike and wave discharges occurred immediately after eye closure. These
discharges did not occur if the room was in darkness (fig. 6). Photic stimulation
evoked occipital spikes and photoconvulsive responses over a range of 6-40 f.sec. with

eyes open and no abnormality with eyes closed. A repeat EEG ten days later showed a sensitivity range of 7-78 f.sec.

### Group D

This small group of 19 patients shows a female/male ratio of 138:100, there being 11 females and 8 males. These patients appear to be the most liable to have fits, the fits occurring with T.V., with flickering light from other sources, and also 'spontaneously'. Seventeen of the 19 show spontaneous spike and wave discharges in their EEGs and 7 show these discharges immediately after eye closure, a higher incidence (37 per cent) than other groups (mean 19 per cent). The incidence of myoclonic jerking during IPS is also highest in this group, 58 per cent compared to 19.5 per cent in the other groups.

*Angela* (18 yrs.) had a tonic-clonic fit while watching T.V. The programme 'Top of the Pops' gave her a giddy feeling and a similar feeling occurred during IPS and also when she looked out of a train window and watched the track going by. She disliked black and white striped patterns. She felt uncomfortable when exposed to flickering sunlight and experienced a 'giddy feeling'. She had an occasional tonic-clonic fit without any evidence of flickering light as a precipitant. Her EEG showed no abnormality until she was exposed to photic stimulation, when photoconvulsive responses were evoked by flash rates between 14 and 24 per second. No abnormality was evoked when she stared at cards carrying a striped black and white pattern.

*Katrina* was first seen at the age of 16, at which time she had myoclonic jerks just after waking in the morning and very rare tonic-clonic fits. She experienced an unpleasant sensation when watching T.V., when looking at the moving steps of escalators and when watching windscreen wipers, and a similar sensation occurred when a photoconvulsive discharge was evoked by photic stimulation. In all she had seven EEGs between the ages of 16 and 25, and five of these showed abnormality on IPS. Myoclonic jerks were evoked by IPS, but no spontaneous abnormality was ever seen in the basic records.

*Andrew* began to have minor attacks, described as absences, at the age of 8 years and he also had tonic-clonic fits. He was referred for an EEG at the age of 16 years, at which time he was reported to be attracted towards the T.V. set. A minor attack was observed prior to the EEG and two similar attacks were evoked by IPS. In the attack his mouth was drawn up on the right, his head and eyes turned to the right and his head jerked. The EEG showed initial sharp waves and polyspikes followed by atypical bilateral 3 c.sec. spike and wave activity for 3 seconds which then slowed to 2 c.sec. and continued for a further 6 seconds. During the attack he could hear but not speak. Some of his attacks were apparently precipitated by bright flickering sunlight. A repeat EEG, six months later, showed spontaneous spike and wave activity which had not been present in the first EEG, but there was no abnormality during IPS even with light of increased intensity. There had been no change in his medication.

### Group E

This group has the highest proportion of female patients, and like Group D contains a significantly larger number of patients with myoclonic epilepsy and with myoclonic jerking evoked by IPS than Groups A, B, C and F. Of the 33 patients 23 were female and 10 male (ratio 230:100).

*Nigel* had his first tonic-clonic fit at the age of 12 years. His brother David, who was two years older, began to have tonic-clonic fits at the age of 14 and had already attended the EEG department. David's EEG had shown slow activity in the posterior regions which appeared to be a subharmonic of the alpha rhythm and was regarded as alpha variant activity. There was also some spiking in the left frontal region and a little spiking was evoked by IPS at 20 f.sec. A repeat EEG at 15 years old, when he was receiving sulthiame, phenytoin and phenobarbitone, showed no spiking either in the basic record or during IPS, but the subharmonic alpha variant activity was still present. At no time was there any history of clinical photosensitivity.

Nigel's EEG showed the same sort of alpha variant activity as David's, but spike and wave discharges were inconstantly evoked by IPS with eyes open and closed. Some months later Nigel had a fit while fishing, probably induced by sunlight on the water. A repeat EEG at the age of 15 showed abnormality only during IPS with eyes closed, the sensitivity range being 17-32 f.sec.

*Gwendoline* (15 yrs.) was referred for EEG because she had 'dizzy spells'. Her basic EEG was normal but IPS evoked occipital spike and also spike and wave discharges. When the latter occurred she experienced the same 'dizzy' sensation as had occurred in the clinical situation for which she was referred, and questioning revealed that many of her 'giddy spells' had been evoked by sunlight shining through trees, on lakes, or at the seaside.

*Mary R* (20 yrs.) had two tonic-clonic fits, one during sleep and one just after waking in the morning. Her EEG showed no significant basic abnormality but IPS evoked spike and wave discharges and generalised myoclonic jerking. On questioning she said that she often felt a 'jittering' sensation when exposed to flickering sunlight.

*Group F*

In these patients there is no evidence of fits having been precipitated by flickering light under everyday circumstances. All have 'spontaneous' fits and some have absences when exposed to the photostimulator in the EEG laboratory. All show photoconvulsive responses. Of the 122 patients, 81 are female and 41 male (ratio 196:100). The mean age of onset is lower than in the other groups. Petit mal is commoner in this group than in the purely light-sensitive groups A and C ($p < .01$), and jerks on photic stimulation are less common in Group F than in all the other groups ($p < .01$).

*Angela* and *Yvonne* (14 yrs.) are identical twins judging from their appearance. Both had a tonic-clonic fit during sleep within the same month and also had their first period at about the same time. EEGs were taken six months later. No abnormality was present in Angela's basic waking record, but when she went to sleep (spontaneously) her EEG showed a little theta spike and wave activity during drowsiness and sleep. Intermittent photic stimulation induced polyspike and wave discharges and some generalised myoclonic jerking with a sensitivity range of 8-28 f.sec. Angela's EEG was taken on the 14th day of her menstrual cycle. Yvonne, on the 4th day of her menstrual cycle, showed no EEG abnormality during waking and she did not go to sleep. Her sensitivity range was 7-50 f.sec. Repeat EEG investigation some months later showed that Angela's sensitivity range was 10-50 f.sec. and Yvonne's was 9-50 f.sec. Their mother's EEG showed no abnormality during IPS. Because myoclonic jerking was evoked by IPS further enquiry was made and a history of early morning jerking was obtained, but there was no evidence that any of the girls' attacks had been precipitated by flickering light. The combination of early morning jerking, rare tonic-clonic fits during sleep, and onset at puberty suggested a diagnosis of myoclonic epilepsy, and a small dose of phenobarbitone was therefore prescribed.

*Caroline* had a minor attack at the age of 7 years in which her eyes rotated upwards, she was unsteady on her feet and she subsequently vomited. She also had brief absences lasting 2-3 seconds. Her EEG showed frequent 3-4 c.sec. spike and wave discharges, but no abnormality was evoked by IPS. Her attacks were controlled with ethosuccimide and phenobarbitone, but a repeat EEG at 9 years showed spike and wave discharges after eye closure and photoconvulsive discharges were evoked by IPS with eyes open. She remained free from fits, but a repeat EEG at the age of 10 years showed right-sided spiking in the basic record, spike and wave discharges after eye closure and a sensitivity range on IPS of 8-62 f.sec. with eyes open. At the age of 12 spontaneous spike and wave discharges were still present after eye closure, but disappeared in the dark. Photoconvulsive responses were still present on IPS. At 14 years spontaneous discharges were still present after eye closure and her sensitivity range was 7-22 f.sec.

*Sharon* was referred for EEG at the age of 16 years, having had tonic-clonic fits since she was 14. During hyperventilation her EEG showed an atypical spike and wave discharge and she fluttered her eyelids and smacked her lips. A similar discharge and temporal lobe absence was evoked by IPS at 20 f.sec., and occurred again when this flash rate was repeated and also at 24 and 28 f.sec.

**Reclassification of groups** (see Table II)

For the purpose of evaluating the findings we have combined Groups A and C, namely, those whose fits have only occurred under the provocation of flickering light in an everyday situation (television or sunlight), as Group I, *Flicker-sensitive*.

Those who have fits with and without flickering light in an everyday situation (B, D, E) are combined as Group II, *Mixed*.

Group III, *'Spontaneous'*, contains patients in F only, whose fits occur without any evidence that they are triggered by a light stimulus. This group show EEG abnormality induced by IPS in the laboratory.

**Subjects who do not have epilepsy**

Twenty-nine relatives of patients with photosensitive epilepsy were investigated. The findings are reported on page 43.

Six patients showed abnormality on IPS, although there was no clinical history of epilepsy. Five of these were male.

*James* (8 yrs.) was referred because of behaviour disorder. There was a past history of febrile convulsions. His basic EEG showed a great deal of 2 c.sec. spike and wave activity and IPS induced occipital spikes. His basic EEG eventually became

## TABLE III
### Close viewers

|  | Close | | Not close | | Not known | | Total | |
|---|---|---|---|---|---|---|---|---|
| Group A | 66 | 60% | 38 | 35% | 6 | 5% | 110 | 100% |
| B | 25 | 34% | 33 | 44% | 16 | 22% | 74 | 100% |
| C | 7 | | 5 | | 1 | | 13 | |
| D | 4 | | 4 | | 7 | | 15 | |
| *Total* | 102 | 48% | 80 | 38% | 30 | 14% | 212 | 100% |

normal with nitrazepam although the behaviour disorder was unaffected, and occipital spikes persisted.

*Stephen* (13 yrs.) also had a behaviour disorder and spike and wave discharges occurred on IPS, the sensitivity range being 14-55 f.sec. The EEG improved with phenytoin, but his behaviour was unchanged.

*Brian* (18 yrs.) was referred for EEG because of headaches. IPS revealed spike and wave with a sensitivity range of 15-23 f.sec. He had sometimes felt a little dizzy when watching T.V.

*Simon* (8 yrs.) had migraine, and IPS evoked spike and wave with a range of 8-20 f.sec.

*Paul* (10 yrs.) had a single symptom—micropsia—and although his basic EEG was normal, spike and wave discharges were evoked on eye closure by flash rates from 10 to 35 per second. The abnormalities disappeared with therapy using sodium valproate, and the EEG remained normal even when the drug was withdrawn. The micropsia was unaffected.

*Amanda* (13 yrs.) the only female in this small group, had a history of syncope and showed occipital spikes and a PCR on eye closure during IPS at rates of 20-28 f.sec.

### Precipitating factors

The commonest precipitant of a fit in a patient with photosensitive epilepsy is undoubtedly viewing television, and this was the responsible factor in 299 of the 454 cases. Nearness to the set appears to be a most important factor—by near is meant a distance of 60 cm. or less. The patient either sits very close to view, or approaches the set to switch channels or adjust the controls.

Table III shows the number of close viewers among 212 patients. At least half the patients were near to the set when their fit occurred. Nearness to the set is a more common factor in Group A than Group B (5 per cent level) and is also commoner in the flicker-sensitive groups A and C than in those with mixed fits, B and D (5 per cent level).

Nearness to the set is certainly not the only factor. Two patients had a fit when looking at a set in a shop window. Another had a fit when the family bought a new set with a larger and brighter screen. One patient had a fit only after prolonged viewing (and spontaneous spike and wave discharges only appeared in this patient's EEG towards the end of the period of testing with IPS). Five patients had their fit when viewing from an angle, but it is very doubtful whether this is a factor and it is more

TABLE IV

| Age in years | 2 | 3 | 4 | 5 | 6 | 7 | 8 | 9 | 10 | 11 | 12 | 13 | 14 | 15 | 16 |
|---|---|---|---|---|---|---|---|---|---|---|---|---|---|---|---|
| No. of males | 2 | 3 | 2 | 2 | 5 | 7 | 14 | 13 | 12 | 14 | 15 | 13 | 17 | 7 | 10 |
| No. of females | 2 | 3 | 3 | 8 | 10 | 10 | 15 | 14 | 25 | 27 | 36 | 25 | 19 | 16 | 10 |
| All cases | 4 | 6 | 5 | 10 | 15 | 17 | 29 | 27 | 37 | 41 | 51 | 38 | 36 | 23 | 20 |

<------------------57---------------> <---------------------------------344-----------
76%

Mean age of onset for males = 14 years. Mean age of onset for females = 13.6 years.
Mean age of onset for all cases = 13.7 years. Mode = 12 years.

probable that they were too near the set. In 6 patients there was clear evidence that the fits induced by T.V. and the EEG abnormality induced by IPS were related to the menstrual cycle.

As yet we have only anecdotal evidence about the effect of colour television. *Pauline* was impulsively attracted to the T.V. screen and would jerk when she was near to the set and then have a tonic-clonic seizure. This behaviour stopped, as did the jerking, when the family bought a colour television set. However, on one occasion when her brother had altered the controls to produce a black and white picture she started to jerk as soon as she went to adjust for colour. She had experienced discomfort when watching 'Top of the Pops' in black and white, but was unaffected when watching it in colour.

We have little evidence, anecdotal or otherwise, of the relation between the type of programme and the occurrence of fits. However, a number of patients have experienced discomfort when viewing the type of programme such as 'Top of the Pops' where 'Op-Art' patterns are used. We have 3 patients who had fits while watching the earlier black and white versions of 'Top of the Pops', and with 2 of them there is EEG confirmation that a combination of flicker and black and white striped patterns evokes a photoconvulsive response.

It is probable that the mechanisms underlying photosensitive epilepsy and pattern epilepsy are essentially similar, so it is not surprising that some of our photosensitive patients also show sensitivity to patterns, usually manifesting itself as an unpleasant sensation. The patterns include the steel steps of escalators, windscreen wipers, railway sleepers and posts viewed from the carriage window, bands formed by fluted glass in windows, roof tiles, striped material, a striped garage door of up-and-over type, a spiromatic toy and the rotating turntable of a record player. The latter is of interest in view of Apuleius' description of vertigo induced by looking at a rotating potter's wheel (p. 4). One child was 'hypnotized' by the yellow, red and white pattern of the kitchen floor.

The commonest source of flickering light other than T.V. is sunlight, either reflected from water, or broken up as the patient travels along an avenue of trees or past railings. Sunlight viewed through fluttering leaves also causes flicker, and sunlight reflected from snow or frost is a rare precipitant of photosensitive epilepsy.

| 17 | 18 | 19 | 20 | 21 | 22 | 23 | 24 | 25 | 26 | 27 | 28 | 29 | 30 | over 30 |
|----|----|----|----|----|----|----|----|----|----|----|----|----|----|---------|
| 8 | 3 | 5 | 2 | 1 |  | 2 | 3 | 1 |  |  | 1 |  |  | 11 |
| 9 | 10 | 7 | 2 | 4 | 5 | 1 | 2 | 2 | 2 | 1 | 1 | 1 | 2 | 9 |
| 17 | 13 | 12 | 4 | 5 | 5 | 3 | 5 | 3 | 2 | 1 | 2 | 1 | 2 | 20 |

`- - - - - - - - - - - - - > < - - - - - - - - - - - - - - - - 53 - - - - - - - - - - - - - - - - - - - - - >`

Reflections from the surface of the water in swimming baths caused fits in 3 patients, and in one case the sunlight was reflected from the roof, the fit occurring while the patient was swimming back-stroke. One boy had a fit while fishing on a sunny day. Flickering sunlight was an epileptogenic factor in 33 patients.

Artificial lights have caused fits in another 22 patients. Four had fits in a fairground or amusement arcade, two in the cinema, and one when watching a home movie. Eight have experienced an unpleasant sensation in discotheques, and another 'felt peculiar' when a pop group suddenly switched on stroboscopes. Reflections from a rotating globe in a dance hall upset one patient, and another 'felt funny' when travelling through an underpass which had lights in the walls. Two patients had fits in supermarkets where there was fluorescent lighting.

## Age of onset

The ages of onset of photosensitive epilepsy are shown in Table IV. The youngest child in whom we have seen a photoconvulsive response was aged 2 years 5 months.

The range of ages is 2-58 years and the mode is at 12 years. The mean age of onset for all cases is 13.7 years, for females is 13.6 years, and for males is 14 years. The age of onset, both average and modal, suggests that puberty plays some part in the genesis of this type of epilepsy, and in 76 per cent of all cases the onset was between the ages of 8 and 19 years.

In 10 cases we had taken EEG records before the onset of photosensitivity. The age at which the EEG showed no abnormality on IPS and the age at which such abnormality was discovered are shown below.

| Age at which EEG showed no abnormality on IPS | Age at which EEG showed PCR on IPS |
|---|---|
| 12, 13, 14 | 17 |
| 15 | 15 yrs. 6 months |
| 7 | 15 |
| 10 | 14 |
| 9 | 12 |
| 9 yrs. 4 months | 9 yrs. 7 months |
| 8 | 9 |
| 7 | 9 |
| 6 | 7 |
| 14 months | 2 yrs. 5 months |

41

## TABLE V
### Sex ratios

|  | Total | Male | Female |
|---|---|---|---|
| General population U.K. 1968 | 55.5m | 100 | 106 |
| Population under 5 years | 4.7m | 100 | 95 |
| Population 5-14 years | 8.6m | 100 | 95 |
| Infantile spasms | 232 | 100 | 50 |
| Febrile convulsions | 280 | 100 | 66 |
| Patients attending for EEG | 1000 | 100 | 75 |
| Temporal lobe epilepsy | 286 | 100 | 79 |
| Tonic-clonic fits | 1545 | 100 | 80 |
| Focal fits | 151 | 100 | 81 |
| Epilepsy clinic (all ages) | 830 | 100 | 82 |
| Impulsive attraction to T.V. | 30 | 100 | 88 |
| Photosensitive epilepsy—Tonic-clonic | 303 | 100 | 148 |
| Abnormality evoked by IPS | 402 | 100 | 163 |
| Petit mal, *not* photosensitive | 16 | 100 | 166 |
| Photosensitive epilepsy—all cases | 454 | 100 | 169 |
| Photosensitive epilepsy—petit mal | 52 | 100 | 189 |
| Jerks evoked by IPS | 97 | 100 | 194 |
| Photosensitive epilepsy—absence induced by IPS | 31 | 100 | 343 |
| Photosensitive epilepsy—myoclonic fits | 39 | 100 | 388 |

A hormonal factor could account for the development of photosensitivity in the first 5 cases above. The girl of 17 was pregnant and the other cases could have been associated with puberty. The girl of 15 years 6 months was at a different point in her menstrual cycle from when the first EEG had been taken.

Two additional siblings are of interest. The girl had spike and wave on IPS at the age of 6 years, and at 10 years had a fit while watching T.V. Her brother had spike and wave on IPS at the age of 3 years and a fit at the age of 8 years.

### Sex

Of the 454 patients with epilepsy, 285 were female and 169 male. In view of the higher proportion of females, which is the opposite of that found in patients with infantile spasms, we have compared various populations. In Table V comparison is made with figures for the general population based on the census results and the Registrar General's estimates for 1968. All the other populations shown in the table had been personally studied by the authors, either because they had been referred for EEG, or because they were part of a research study. Comparative figures from the literature are shown in Table VI.

It can be seen that while males predominate in infantile spasms and to a lesser extent in febrile convulsions, the proportion of females in patients with tonic-clonic fits, temporal lobe epilepsy and focal fits is a little less than in the normal population. The proportion in these latter types of epilepsy is similar to the proportion of females in an unselected consecutive group of patients attending for EEG examination, and in an unselected group of patients of all ages attending an epilepsy clinic.

TABLE VI

**TABLE VI**
**Sex ratios from the literature**

|  | Male | Female |
|---|---|---|
| Gowers—all epilepsy | 100 | 108 |
| Lennox—all epilepsy | 100 | 82 |
| Rutter *et al.*—epilepsy 5-14 yrs. | 100 | 87 |
| Lennox—petit mal | 100 | 127 |
| Gibberd—petit mal | 100 | 178 |

**TABLE VII**
**Sex ratios in Groups A - F**

|  | Male | Female |
|---|---|---|
| Group A | 100 | 158 |
| Group B | 100 | 160 |
| Group C | 100 | 110 |
| Group D | 100 | 138 |
| Group E | 100 | 230 |
| Group F | 100 | 196 |
| All cases | 100 | 169 |

On the other hand, the proportion of females is higher in all cases of photo-sensitive epilepsy, regardless of type of fit induced by IPS, in all patients showing abnormal discharges evoked by IPS, in all patients in whom IPS evoked myoclonic jerking, and all patients with true petit mal. This latter finding is confirmed by Lennox (1960) and Gibberd (1966). It will be noted that the highest proportion of females occurs in those patients with photosensitive epilepsy whose induced fits are either petit mal absences or myoclonic jerks, and also that myoclonic jerking evoked by IPS is commoner in females. It is interesting that 77 per cent of the 31 patients in whom an absence was induced by IPS were female. The group of patients who are impulsively attracted to the T.V. screen are the only photosensitive patients to show the same sex ratio as the non-photosensitive patients with epilepsy. The difference in the sex ratios of the impulsively-attracted group and the absence-induced group is highly significant (0.1 per cent). These patients are discussed in detail later (page 49). Two patients had absences induced by IPS and were also impulsively attracted to the T.V. and are therefore excluded from the statistical calculations.

Table VII shows the proportion of females in Groups A-F. The differences appear to be due to the proportion of tonic-clonic fits in relation to other types of fits and to the distribution of the cases where IPS induced an absence. Thus the higher proportion of females in Groups E and F appears to be due to the high incidence of petit mal, myoclonic epilepsy and absence-induced cases.

**Family history**

Thirty-seven patients had a family history of photosensitive epilepsy. This is not surprising since the EEG abnormality characteristic of photosensitive epilepsy is 3 c.sec. spike and wave activity, and the studies of Metrakos and Metrakos (1960, 1961, 1966, 1969) suggest that this abnormality is due to an autosomal dominant gene.

There were three pairs of 'identical' twins, two female and one male. There were 17 families with more than one affected member, the affected relatives in these 17 families being as follows:

| | |
|---|---|
| Siblings | 11 |
| Parent and child | 4 |
| Cousin | 1 |
| Parent and child and sibling | 1 |

In four cases we did not have complete information about the proband's affected sibling or parent, but in 9 cases siblings and parents belonged to different clinical groups (e.g. one member of the family might have fits only with T.V., while the other only had spontaneous fits). In four families both siblings were in the same clinical group. We carried out EEG investigation of 17 siblings or parents of these patients, and also investigated the relatives of 3 other photo-sensitive patients. Another 5 patients had relatives who said they disliked flickering light and we examined 7 of these relatives. Thus we examined 29 relatives in all. Abnormal EEGs were found in non-epileptic siblings in only two families.

The three pairs of identical twins are of interest. *Elizabeth* had tonic-clonic seizures during sleep but a normal basic waking EEG, and spike and wave discharges with associated myoclonic jerks were evoked by IPS. Her sensitivity range at the age of eight was 8-13 f.sec. with eyes open. At 9 years the range was 13-17 f.sec. Her sister *Susan* does not have any fits, but at age 9 she had similar spike and wave discharges and jerks on IPS, with a sensitivity range 16-18. Five months later the effect of coloured photic stimulation was tested. Elizabeth had occipital spikes only and Susan showed no abnormality at all. Their responses were therefore very similar.

*Angela* and *Yvonne* have had tonic-clonic seizures during sleep and myoclonic jerks just after waking, the onset of epilepsy being in the same month. There is no evidence that flickering light has precipitated any attack. Both girls have photo-convulsive responses and myoclonic jerks during IPS. On two occasions their sensitivity ranges were essentially similar and on another occasion the ranges were different, probably because they were at different points in their menstrual cycles. Their mother has a normal EEG. The most recent investigation showed Yvonne to have spike and wave responses to IPS with eyes open and no abnormality with eyes closed, while Angela showed the reverse.

*David* weighed 1.76 Kg. at birth and *Kevin's* weight was 2.44 Kg. and they have subsequently showed physical differences in height and weight. Both have spontaneous absences with no clinical evidence of photosensitivity. David shows no spike and wave in his basic EEG, but a 5 second discharge of atypical spike and wave was evoked by IPS. Kevin's basic record shows a spike and wave discharge similar in appearance and duration to that shown by David, but occurring spontaneously, and there is no abnormality on IPS (fig. 7). Similarity of spike and wave discharges evoked by IPS is not confined to twins. Figure 8 shows a typical photoconvulsive response induced in a brother and sister.

44

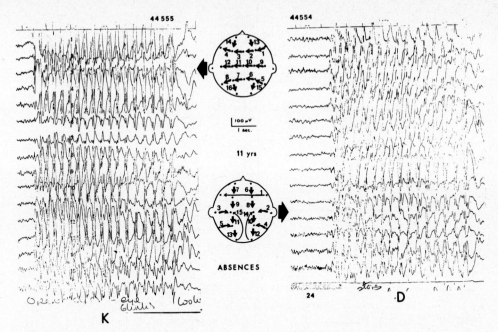

**Fig. 7.** Spike and wave discharges in 'identical' twins. The discharge of twin K occurred spontaneously, whereas that of D was evoked by IPS at 24 f.sec. The discharges, however, are very similar, as is the background EEG.

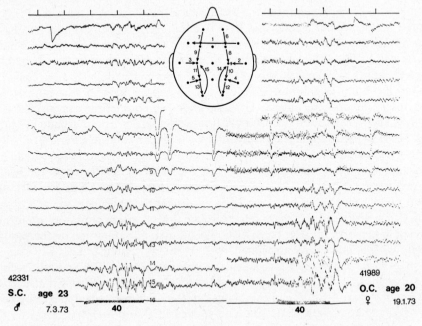

**Fig. 8.** EEG discharges evoked by the same flash rate (40 f.sec.) in brother and sister.

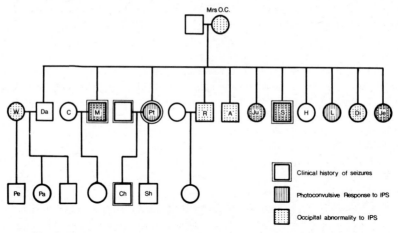

**Fig. 9.** Inheritance of photosensitivity in family 'C' . (From Herrick 1973.)

Clinical history of seizures

Photoconvulsive Response to IPS

Occipital abnormality to IPS

Three other families are of particular interest. Family C (fig. 9) consists of 12 children, one of whom (a boy) died in infancy. The 11 survivors all had a detailed EEG examination including investigations of visual evoked potentials (VEP) using a computer of average transients (CAT). Of the 5 surviving boys, two (M and S), had a fit whilst watching television. Their basic records were normal but both showed spike and wave on IPS. Three boys (A aged 17, R aged 18, and D aged 27) have no history of fits. Their basic EEGs are normal, but A showed occipital spikes in the VEP and R had one episode of occipital slow waves during IPS. C (the wife of M) has a normal EEG; we have not taken the EEG of their infant son. W (the wife of Da) has occipital spikes and her mother may have had fits. Her first child (Pe) is not the son of her husband Da but the other two children are, and her first and second children have normal EEGs, although her infant child has not been investigated. Pt had a fit while watching T.V. when she was 12. She has a normal basic record but spike and wave on IPS. Both the children of Pt (Ch. aged 3 and Sh. aged 2) have normal basic EEGs and no abnormality on IPS. The elder child, who has febrile convulsions, is the son of Pt and her husband (who suffers from epilepsy), but the husband is not the father of the younger child. The EEG responses to IPS are shown in Figure 10. All the other 5 girls have normal basic records. Ju, aged 16, L aged 12 and Je aged 10 all have spike and wave on IPS though none has ever had a fit. H, aged 13, has no abnormality on IPS but Di, aged 11, has occipital spikes in the VEP. Mrs OC, aged 48, has no abnormality in her basic EEG but occipital abnormality on IPS.

*S.G.,* a girl aged 12, had fits provoked by television and was impulsively attracted to the T.V. set. Her basic EEG was normal, but abnormal discharges were evoked by IPS and were associated with a 'funny feeling'. The EEG of her nine-year-old sister showed photoconvulsive responses during IPS and also occipital spikes, but she had had no fits and did not experience any discomfort with IPS or with T.V. Another sister aged 16 had complained of feeling 'funny' when in a discotheque where flashing lights were used. She also showed PCR and occipital spikes on IPS. Their mother refused an EEG.

46

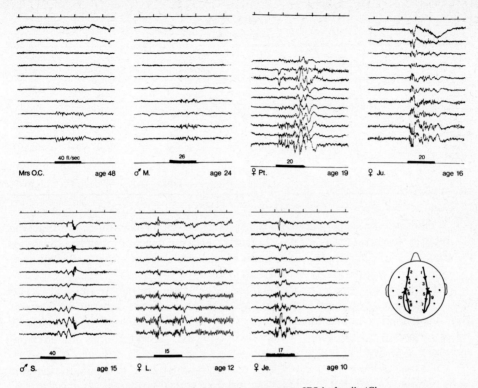

**Fig. 10.** Samples of abnormal responses to IPS in family 'C'.

*M.T.,* aged 36, had fits precipitated by flickering sunlight (Group E), and IPS evoked 3 c.sec. spike and wave discharges which persisted for some seconds after the flicker had stopped. Her mother had epilepsy, but we were unable to discover whether she had been photosensitive and she had never had an EEG. *S.T.,* the 12-year-old daughter of M.T. by her first marriage, had spontaneous fits and also showed impulsive attraction to the T.V. set (Group B). Her EEG showed persistent spike and wave activity with an associated absence, evoked by IPS. *E.T.,* aged 10, is the daughter of M.T. by her second husband, and has petit mal absences but is not clinically photosensitive (Group F). Her EEG shows persistent spike and wave discharges evoked by IPS with associated absences. Finally, *A.T.,* a son aged 5, has spontaneous fits and is impulsively attracted to the T.V. set (Group B). His EEG shows spike and wave discharges during IPS and a great deal of spontaneous spike and wave activity. It should be mentioned that all the above members of the family show some spontaneous spike and wave discharges. S.T. is now married, and her two infant sons have normal EEGs.

**Types of fit**

One cannot always obtain an accurate description of the fit, especially its mode of onset, but it is usually possible to establish whether the patient fell to the ground or

## TABLE VIII
### Types of fit

| Type of fit | Group I (Flicker-sensitive) | | Group II (Mixed) | | Group III (Spontaneous) | |
|---|---|---|---|---|---|---|
| | No. | % | No. | % | No. | % |
| Tonic-clonic | 152 | 84 | 83 | 55 | 68 | 56 |
| Minor-absence | 11 | 6 | 23 | 15 | 25 | 20 |
| Myoclonic only | 3 | 1.5 | 12 | 8 | 2 | 1.5 |
| Partial-focal | 5 | 2.5 | 2 | 1 | 4 | 3.5 |
| Mixed | 11 | 6 | 31 | 21 | 23 | 19 |
| Total cases | 181 | 100 | 115 | 100 | 122 | 100 |
| Myoclonic ± other fits | 4 | 2 | 23 | 14 | 12 | 10 |

not. A description of true petit mal absences may be obtained in those children who are impulsively attracted to the television screen because the child's behaviour arouses the attention of the parent. Partial seizures are uncommon, but of particular interest.

We have classified the types of fit as follows:

(a) *Generalised seizures of tonic-clonic type.* These are mostly classical Grand Mal, but include any patient known to have fallen unconscious, any patient who was incontinent even if falling did not occur, and patients with brief bilateral clonic attacks associated with some disturbance of consciousness (differentiated from myoclonic as defined below).

(b) *Minor seizures* with no motor manifestations other than slight rhythmic eyelid movements. Most of the minor seizures were typical absences. Absences during which lip-smacking, mouthing, fumbling or orientation movements occurred were also classified as minor attacks, as were attacks where there was some alteration of awareness and subjective sensation, but no motor phenomena.

(c) *Bilateral myoclonic jerks* without disturbance of consciousness. Patients were placed in this category if this was the only type of fit. Patients who had myoclonic jerking leading to a generalised tonic-clonic fit were classified under (e).

(d) *Partial seizures* with focal clonic convulsions, or psychomotor attacks.

(e) *Mixed epilepsy* in which several types of attack occurred at various times. A patient who had tonic-clonic fits precipitated by television viewing, but other types of fit at other times, would be included in this group. Most of the patients who had more than one type of fit showed a combination of tonic-clonic fits and minor fits, the next most common combination being myoclonic fits and generalised tonic-clonic seizures.

Table VIII shows the distribution of fits in relation to the three clinical groups.

*Tonic-clonic* fits are the most common in all groups, but show the highest incidence in Group I.

*Minor* fits are rare in the purely flicker-sensitive patients and commonest in Group III, the difference being significant at the 1 per cent level. Patients in Group II were also more likely to have minor fits than those in Group I (p < .01).

*Myoclonic* jerks without a history of tonic-clonic fits at any time were rare. If one includes those patients who had an occasional generalised tonic-clonic seizure—usually though not always preceded by myoclonic jerking—the total number of patients with bilateral myoclonic jerks is 39 (9 per cent of all cases). The highest incidence is in Group II and the lowest in Group I. The important factor appears to be the tendency to spontaneous fits, and the difference in incidence of myoclonic epilepsy in Group I and in Groups II and III is highly significant.

One would expect generalized seizures—whether they are tonic-clonic, absences, or myoclonic jerks—to be more common, because bilateral 3 c.sec. spike and wave discharges often occur during IPS. Of special interest, therefore, are those patients in whom flickering light provokes focal, psychomotor or temporal lobe fits, or a peculiar sensation. *Focal motor seizures* were induced by television in 6 patients, and by flickering sunlight in one patient. A psychomotor fit occurred in 5 patients, preceded by nausea or a 'funny taste' in the mouth. Three patients experienced peculiar subjective sensations—usually unpleasant, but difficult to describe—while watching T.V. or in flickering sunlight, and three of them felt the same sensation during IPS. Another patient in whom a diagnosis of epilepsy had not been made experienced a 'giddy' feeling during IPS, coinciding with every discharge of spike and wave, and recognised this feeling as the same as her 'giddy spells'. Questioning revealed that these spells were evoked by flickering sunlight.

One patient who experienced a peculiar sensation while fishing on a sunny day, and then had a fit, recognised the same sensation during IPS.

Four patients who had 'spontaneous' tonic-clonic fits also experienced a peculiar sensation ('dizzy', 'giddy', 'funny') when close to the T.V. screen and three of these patients felt the same sensation during IPS.

The sensations described above are not those of fear or apprehension which may be felt by some patients when they are placed in the laboratory situation of being exposed to a photostimulator.

### Impulsive attraction to T.V. screen

Thirty patients are impulsively attracted to the T.V. screen. Often the parents use the terms 'hypnotised', 'fascinated' or 'drawn like a magnet towards the set'. In some patients the attraction of the screen is so great that as soon as they observe the television they are drawn inexorably towards it. Some children appear to enjoy the sensation evoked, while most do not wish to go near the set but are unable to stop themselves. We have not always found it possible to assess whether this attraction to the set has or has not been subject to voluntary control and whether it has evoked a pleasurable sensation. Patients who do not approach the set voluntarily can usually be treated by the monocular method, and merely have to cover their eyes with the palm of their hand (see p. 96). The others will not respond to this method, and have to wear an eye patch throughout the period of television viewing. Even then it is unwise to leave the child alone in the room while the T.V. set is on, since the attraction may be so great that he will remove the eye patch.

Of these 30 patients, 16 are male and 14 female. As has already been mentioned (p. 43), this ratio is significantly different (5 per cent level) from that of the other photosensitive patients, and in comparison with the patients in whom IPS induces an absence the difference is much greater (0.1 per cent level). This latter group of patients tend to have narrow sensitivity ranges (see page 65), whereas the impulsively

49

attracted group have wider ranges. This difference is significant at the 1 per cent level. The high proportion of wide ranges may indicate that these patients are more at risk from flicker.

Eighteen of these patients are flicker-sensitive only, belonging to Group I. The remaining 12 all have spontaneous fits. Sixteen have tonic-clonic fits, 6 have absences, 2 have myoclonic jerks only, and 6 have mixed fits. As might be expected, of the 26 tested all but one were more sensitive to IPS with eyes open than with eyes closed. Twenty-four showed spontaneous spike and wave discharges in their basic EEG, which is a significantly higher (5 per cent) proportion than the other patients and may be a further indication that this small group of patients are particularly at risk.

It has been suggested (Harley *et al.* 1967, Andermann 1971) that these patients are similar to those rare patients who induce fits in themselves by waving their hand across their eyes, or by blinking, while staring at a source of bright light. In two of our cases there was enough evidence to suggest that the children were using the T.V. screen as a flickering light source. One of them used to go up to the set in the middle of a programme and switch channels for no apparent reason. Three other children may have used the T.V. screen as a stimulator. In the remaining 25 patients there was no evidence to suggest self-induction of epilepsy.

Comparison of our impulsively attracted group with the series described by Andermann *et al.* (1962) is difficult, because they did not give details of the techniques used, nor is there any differentiation between patients with normal basic EEGs and those showing spontaneous spike and wave. The sex ratio of their patients shows a 2:1 preponderance of females (M:F = 100:233) which is similar to the ratio in our other photosensitive groups, but quite different from our impulsive group (M:F = 100:86). Andermann *et al.* give a much higher incidence of petit mal than we find and comparison is shown below. The figures are *inclusive* since most of the cases described by Andermann *et al.* had two or more types of fit.

| Type of fit | Impulsively attracted to T.V. screen | Self-induced (Andermann et al. 1962) |
|---|---|---|
| Tonic-clonic | 22 | 9 |
| Petit mal | 9 | 17 |
| Myoclonic | 2 | 13 |

It is, of course, possible that the difference may depend on classification of type of fit.

We have only 5 patients who appear to induce fits by hand waving.

*R.M.* (10 yrs.) is educationally subnormal and has minor fits. His basic EEG shows spike and wave discharges and IPS evoked photoconvulsive discharges and associated myoclonic jerks. *D.G.* (11 yrs.) is also educationally subnormal and has minor attacks. Her basic EEG is normal, but spike and wave discharges and myoclonic jerks were evoked by IPS. *A.W.* (10 yrs.) originally had infantile spasms and subsequently developed tonic-clonic fits, which occurred spontaneously and were also evoked by T.V. In addition he had attacks apparently evoked by hand-waving in sunlight. He is retarded. His EEG shows considerable basic abnormality with slow waves and spikes, and a PCR was evoked following eye closure during IPS at 20 f.sec.

M.A. (11 yrs.) is subnormal and was in a state of minor status at the time of the EEG. It was quite clear that his hand waving was part of his seizure and that he was not evoking attacks by staring at a bright light in the laboratory. The degree of spontaneous abnormality was so great that he was given oral barbiturate which reduced the spontaneous abnormality in about 20 minutes and made it possible to test the effect of photo stimulation. Polyspike and wave discharges were evoked and there was no reduction in abnormality when monocular stimulation was tested. The fifth patient, Jamil K., has already been described (page 34). He had major fits induced by TV. and flickering sunlight, and also minor attacks and myoclonic jerks. He is sensitive to patterns. His basic EEG is normal. He attends a normal school. His response to IPS is now normal and he has had no attacks since receiving sodium valproate.

# CHAPTER 6

# Laboratory Studies: EEG and IPS

**EEG method**

The laboratory studies in this section were carried out in three departments. The first two (Dudley Road Hospital and Birmingham Children's Hospital) are clinical EEG departments, while the third (The Neuropsychology Unit, University of Aston) is a University unit involved in clinical research into EEG and visual evoked potentials. All departments use essentially similar methods of investigation, and many of the staff interchange between the three departments. Computer facilities are, however, only available at the Neuropsychology Unit where the more complex studies were carried out.

Most of the EEG records were made either on a 16-channel Elema Schönander machine or an 8 or 12-channel S.L.E. machine. In the early studies Elther or Offner machines were used.

Scalp silver-silver chloride disc electrodes were placed according to the International 10/20 system (Jasper 1958). In some cases additional sub-occipital electrodes were used when the spatial distribution of occipital spikes was investigated.

A routine resting record was taken of all patients on each occasion. For the initial investigation a number of montages were used, including parasagittal, bi-temporal and transverse montage. Hyperventilation was performed for 2½ or 3 minutes. On subsequent investigations the number of montages used in the resting record was reduced, but on each occasion a parasagittal montage was recorded.

The response to photic stimulation was recorded on either a parasagittal montage or a modified parasagittal montage, including right occipital ($O_2$) to right Rolandic ($C_4$), and left occipital ($O_1$) to left Rolandic ($C_3$) derivations. During investigations of the spatial distribution of occipital spikes a special VEP montage (fig. 11) was used (Harding *et al.* 1969).

At the Dudley Road Hospital Department advantage was taken of the high paper speeds (15 or 30 cm./sec.) (fig. 11) available on the Elema Schönander machine to allow measurement of the latency of the occipital spikes directly from the basic record. During this part of the investigation the gain of the EEG system was increased from 100 $\mu$/cm. to 50, 30 or 20 $\mu$/cm. In making this type of measurement the alignment of the ink jets must be extremely accurate. The output of the photo-stimulator was monitored using a photocell placed on the patient's left shoulder. In all recordings the overall time constant of the system was 0.3 seconds.

**Findings in basic EEG**

The basic EEG includes the response to hyperventilation. Only 3 categories have been distinguished:

(a) normal records;

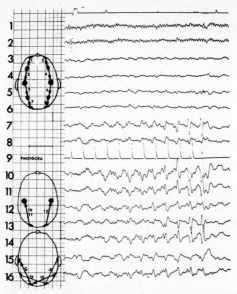

**Fig. 11.** Occipital spikes at fast paper speed (15 cm.sec.). Standard parasagittal in upper 8 channels with occipital spikes shown in channels 7 and 8. Flash rate (channel 9) is 9 f.sec. Channels 10-16 show special VEP montage with occipital spikes. Ch. 10 = 70 $\mu$v/cm, all other channels = $\mu$/cm. (From Panayiotopoulos *et al.* 1972.)

(b) non-specific abnormality (unilateral or bilateral slow waves or other mild abnormalities);

(c) abnormal records including spikes and spike and wave discharges.

We do not regard the non-specific abnormalities as being significant in relation to photosensitivity, so have combined them with the normal records. The total number of normal and non-specific records is 201.

Spikes were rarely seen (8 cases) and the commonest abnormality was bilateral spike and wave. We have not differentiated the various types of spike and wave discharge, but have included under this heading the classical 3 c.sec. spike and wave, atypical spike and wave with slow waves at frequencies other than 3 c.sec. and discharges which are bilaterally asymmetrical or asynchronous.

Spike and wave discharges and spikes were seen in 253 of the epileptic patients (54 per cent). There was little difference in the individual groups, the figure for Group I being 50 per cent, for Group II 58 per cent, and for Group III 54 per cent.

Of the 253 patients with spike and wave or spikes (in future these cases will be referred to as abnormal, and the normal and non-specific cases as normal), 90 (36 per cent) showed spike and wave discharges immediately following eye closure. These spike and wave discharges were sometimes associated with brief fluttering of the eyelids or a slight generalised myoclonic jerk. The discharges were not usually present in total darkness (see fig. 6). Their presence in the basic record almost invariably

53

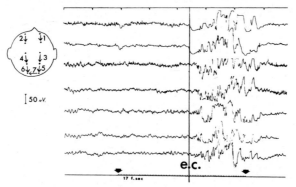

**Fig. 12.** The effect of eye closure during IPS. Arrow indicates onset and end of train of flashes at 17 per second. (From Jeavons 1969.)

indicates that abnormalities will be evoked by IPS and thus they act as a good warning sign for the EEG technician. These discharges involve all regions and must be distinguished from a physiological response to eye closure which consists of high amplitude slow waves confined to the posterior regions, often seen in children during hyperventilation. In addition, the act of eye closure is frequently followed by 'squeak', i.e. activity which is 2 c.sec. faster than the basic alpha rhythm (see page 22, where the importance of differentiating the act of eye closure from the state of the eyes is discussed). Figure 12 shows the effect of eye closure during IPS at 17 f.sec.

In a very few cases 'spontaneous' spike and wave discharges occurred only after the patient had been exposed to IPS. In these cases further testing was stopped and on one or two occasions the patient was given an oral anticonvulsant. Although we have no proof that such patients were developing increased sensitivity owing to the accumulated effect of IPS we did not feel justified in exposing the patient to any risk. One of these patients had once had a fit after very prolonged T.V. viewing. We rated patients as showing abnormal basic EEGs only if spike and wave occurred prior to IPS, so the above patients were not included in this category. In one patient eye closure was followed by spike and wave discharges, but there was no abnormality whatsoever on IPS.

One patient produced spike and wave discharges on changing the direction of gaze. The discharge was not due to blinking.

One boy of seven showed spike and wave discharges when he opened his eyes, and had an associated myoclonic jerk. This happened on two separate occasions. During IPS with eyes open he showed spike and wave and jerks, but no abnormality with closed eyes.

### Photic stimulation methods

In our initial studies of photosensitive epilepsy our first concern was to develop a technique which would allow accurate establishment of the range of flash rates to which a patient was sensitive (including both occipital spikes and the photoconvulsive response), under various standard conditions. It was essential that the method was

54

safe, and indeed one of our aims was to avoid causing any discomfort or distress to the patients, and to develop a technique which had a very low probability of inducing a tonic-clonic fit.

To some extent all such investigations must be a compromise. It is important to establish the range of flash rates to which the patient is sensitive both with eyes open and eyes closed, to compare binocular and monocular stimulation, and to investigate the effect of lateral gaze and lateral illumination and of pattern superimposed on the stimulus. However, in order to avoid distress to the patient it has frequently been necessary to restrict the duration of a train of stimuli, the number of such trains and the total amount of exposure to IPS.

EEG responses to photic stimulation appear to depend on two main factors—the relative brightness of the photostimulator in comparison to the background illumination, and the total number of retinal cells which are being activated. These two factors must be either controlled or systematically varied during the investigation. The type of photostimulator used is the modern electronic stroboscope with a gas discharge lamp. Photostimulators produce a blue/white flash of extremely short duration, usually between 10 and 30 $\mu$/sec. The intensity of the flash is between 400 and 10,000 candelas per square metre (nits). Methods of measuring the intensity of photostimulators are not uniform and many manufacturers specify energy (Joules) rather than the actual luminance of the stimulator. Although comparison of photostimulators might at first sight appear to be simple, in our experience it proved difficult and we tried several physical methods before deciding to use photometry (see page 109).

To standardise the spatial distribution of the luminance of the visual field the photostimulator was placed 30 cm. directly in front of the patient's eyes. The size of the photostimulator of course affects the spatial distribution of the luminance; the two types we used, the Kaiser and the Grass, subtended 28° and 24.5° visual angle respectively.

Photostimulators also vary in the degree to which the light is diffused by the front glass. Some photostimulators are fitted with a ground glass screen, others with a frosted or patterned glass. Obviously the degree of diffusion affects the relative intensity of the light falling on the retina and also its uniformity. In many of our studies we controlled this factor by using a true diffusing screen.

The original Kaiser photostimulator was unique in having a metallic protective grid lying behind the glass. This grid presents a pattern to the patient, thus increasing the contrast and contours within the area of the stimulus. This important factor is discussed in the next chapter. Photostimulators vary in the range of flash rates which they will deliver; most will deliver flash rates over a range of 1-50 f.sec., but some are capable of delivering flashes up to 100 f.sec. This higher range has allowed us to measure the upper limit of flash rate sensitivity, but it should be noted that on many photostimulators the deliverance of flashes at this rate appears to be subject to some errors, and at high rates subharmonic variations of the flash pulses in terms of amplitude are produced. This tendency appears to be related to the age of the flash tube.

The patient is usually in a comfortable reclining or horizontal position. The level of background illumination is usually controlled by excluding day light and using the artificial room light. In some rooms it was possible to vary the artificial lighting by dimming. The effectiveness of photic stimulation is of course enhanced when the room is in darkness since the relative brightness of the flickering light is increased. However, a darkened room does not allow clear observation of any behavioural responses which the patient may make.

Placing the lamp 30 cm. from the outer canthus of the patient's eyes enabled the lamp to subtend a large proportion of the visual field, while allowing us to observe the patient's face and eyelids to see whether the eyes were properly open or closed, and whether the patient was looking straight at the lamp (fig. 32). It is essential that the lamp is directly in front of the patient's eyes, except where the effect of lateral stimulation is being investigated. It is helpful if the circular diffusion screen of the lamp is marked in the centre with a small hollow circle at which the patient is instructed to look. The patient is told exactly what to do and exactly what is going to happen, so that one can compare the first occasion of stimulation with subsequent ones. Surprise should play no part in the investigation.

The patient is tested with one frequency of photic stimulation at a time, and the length of photic stimulation is pre-determined. We commonly use two seconds of photic stimulation, and this period is controlled by an automatic trigger circuit which allows the stimulation to be stopped by the investigator immediately a photoconvulsive response is obtained. The patient is tested under the following conditions:

(a) with eyes kept open;
(b) with eyes kept closed;
(c) during the act of eye closure.

The latter condition is only used when responses are not obtained under the first two conditions, or where direct comparison of the three conditions is important. In the first part of the investigation the patient keeps his eyes open and photic stimulation is given at appropriate flash rates. The patient then keeps his eyes closed and the test is repeated.

When it is necessary to investigate the effect of eye closure photic stimulation is commenced with the patient's eyes open and then after 5 seconds of stimulation the patient closes his eyes and stimulation continues for a further 5 seconds.

In all these investigations, it was our common practice to use flicker at 20 f.sec. as an initial screening flash rate. This rate will induce an abnormal response in 84 per cent of photosensitive patients (but see page 71). In the initial screening the 20 f.sec. stimulation was given for 5 seconds, then the patient was asked to close his eyes and photic stimulation continued for a further 5 seconds. If no abnormality occurred during the whole of this ten-second exposure to flicker, the same procedure was used for the following flash rates: 24, 16, 12, 10, 8, 6, 4, 3, 2 and 1 f.sec. If abnormal discharges were evoked by the initial test flash rate, either with the eyes open or on eye closure, the following method was used. The patient kept his eyes open throughout the testing and the period of flash was limited to two seconds, or less if a photoconvulsive response occurred. Testing was commenced at low flash rates, usually starting at one flash per second and progressing upwards in steps of 1 f.sec. until abnormality was consistently evoked. Stimulation was then given at a high flash

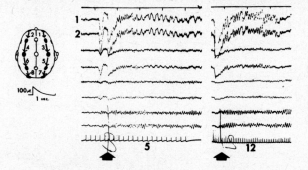

**Fig. 13.** Photomyoclonic response, occurring when the eyes are closed. The anterior response to IPS at 5 and 12 f.sec. can be clearly observed in channels 1 and 2. (From Jeavons 1969.)

rate, usually starting at 80 f.sec. and reducing in steps of 10 f.sec. until abnormality occurred. The upper limit of sensitivity was then established by varying the flash rate in steps of two flashes per second.

In view of the findings described later in this chapter (see page 69) we have modified our technique of IPS. The initial test frequency is 16 f.sec. and subsequent testing is carried out at 1, 3, 5, 7, 9, 11, 13, 15, 17, 19, 21, 25 and 50 f.sec. The use of odd numbers for the lower flash rates is to simplify the problems of subharmonic and harmonic components of photic driving. Twenty-five and 50 f.sec. are used to match the flicker rates of T.V. screens in Europe (in countries with a mains frequency of 60 Hz., the flash rates should be 30 and 60 per second).

### EEG responses to photic stimulation

From the clinical point of view photic stimulation is of value mainly in the identification of the photosensitive patient.

The responses to IPS can be classed as follows on the basis of their EEG distribution:

   (a) The response is seen only in the *anterior* regions: photomyoclonic responses;
   (b) The response is seen only in the *posterior* regions: photic driving, visual evoked potentials (VEP), occipital spikes;
   (c) The response is widespread, bilateral, and involves *anterior and posterior* regions: photoconvulsive responses.

*Photomyoclonic responses*

We have only seen these in two patients (fig. 13). Our technique is extremely unlikely to elicit this physiological phenomenon, which only occurs when the eyes are closed and the light is extremely bright or very close to the eyes—two conditions which we avoid.

*Photic driving*

These physiological responses are of scientific interest, but abnormalities of photic driving rarely give information which is not already manifest in the basic record. Photic driving responses may be at fundamental, harmonic or subharmonic rates. Rarely the combination of fundamental and harmonic rates produces a

57

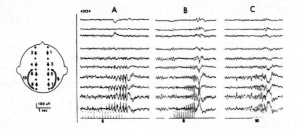

**Fig. 14.** Occipital spikes evoked by IPS at 5, 8 and 10 f.sec. The posterior distribution of the spikes can be clearly observed in channels 5-10. At 8 and 10 f.sec. the occipital spikes are followed by an ill-defined PCR.

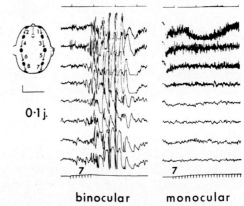

**Fig. 15.** Photoconvulsive response, mainly at 3 c.sec., evoked by IPS at 7 f.sec. by the Kaiser photostimulator at intensity 0.1 Joule. The abnormal response is not evoked when one eye is covered, even though the train of stimuli is longer. Calibration 100 μv and 1 second.

binocular          monocular

pseudo-spike and wave appearance, which on visual inspection is very similar to negative occipital spikes and which can only be differentiated with certainty by using an averaging computer.

*Occipital spikes*

These occur at the same rate as the flash and are electro-negative to the occipital electrode (fig. 14). They may be seen alone or may precede a photoconvulsive response. When seen alone they probably do not indicate epilepsy, but in isolation they are rare and we are uncertain of their clinical significance. Of 45 patients who showed occipital spikes alone in response to IPS, only two had photosensitive epilepsy and 22 had a history of epilepsy of various types (including two with a past history of febrile convulsions). In the remaining 21 patients there was no evidence of epilepsy. Ten had syncopal attacks, 3 showed behaviour disorder, 4 had headaches, and 3 had had a cerebrovascular accident. There was one patient with Friedreich's ataxia (Maheshwari and Jeavons 1975). Occipital spikes were seen in 179 out of 280 cases (64 per cent) in our series. They are discussed in detail on page 85.

*Photoconvulsive responses*

Photoconvulsive responses are seen in all regions but show considerable variation, and several types of response may be seen in the same patient on the same occasion. The responses may be accompanied by myoclonic jerking.

There are 6 types of photoconvulsive responses:
1. Bursts of spike and wave activity, usually with a slow component at 3 c.sec. (fig. 15);

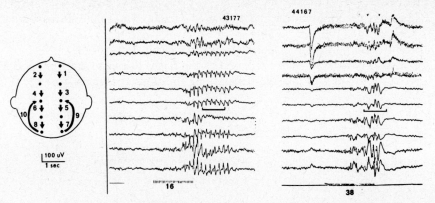

**Fig. 16.** Theta spike and wave at 5 c.sec. in response to 16 f.sec. and irregular theta spike and wave in response to 38 f.sec.

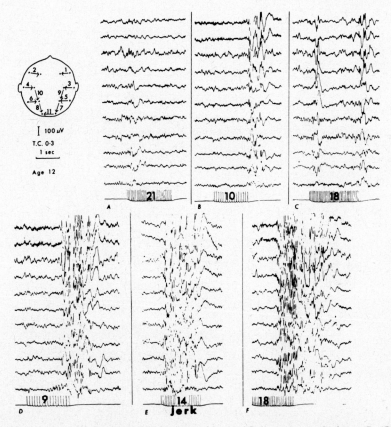

**Fig. 17.** A variety of responses to IPS in one patient. A, 'On' response to 21 f.sec.; B, 'Off' response to 10 f.sec.; C, 'On' and 'Off' response to 18 f.sec.; D, Polyspike and wave response to 9 f.sec.; E, 3 c.sec. spike and wave response with myoclonic jerk to 14 f.sec.; f, Initial polyspikes followed by 3 c.sec. spike and wave to 18 f.sec. Note that in B, D, and F the PCR persists for one second after the cessation of IPS.

2. Bursts of high amplitude theta waves (4-7 c.sec.) with spikes (theta spike and wave) (fig. 16);
3. Bursts of polyspikes or polyspike and wave (fig. 17);
4. Bursts of spikes at the same rate as the flash, distinguished from occipital spikes by the fact that they extend into the anterior regions (figs. 18, 19);

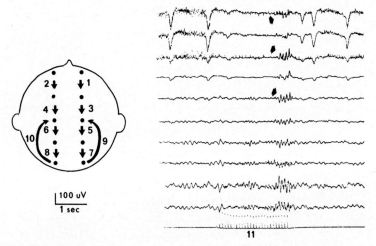

**Fig. 18.** Bursts of spikes at the same rate (11 per sec.) as the flash. Note that spikes extend to the anterior regions, though in this case they are asymmetric (arrowed).

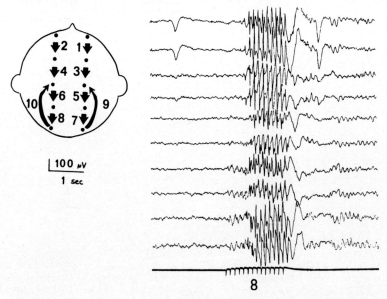

**Fig. 19.** Photoconvulsive response of spike and wave at the same rate (8 per sec.) as the flash.

5. Discharges of 3 c.sec. spike and wave activity lasting more than 5 seconds after the flashing has ceased, and associated with a clinical absence (fig. 20);
6. Bilateral high amplitude slow waves without spikes, seen through all regions.

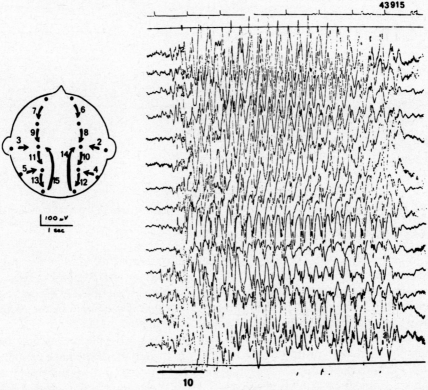

**Fig. 20.** Clinical absence, with 3 c.sec. spike and wave discharge lasting 6 seconds. IPS at 10 f.sec. indicated by bar.

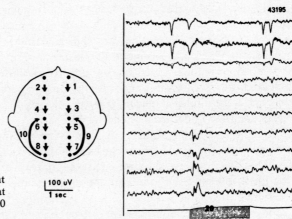

**Fig. 21.** Exaggerated VEP, only present in occipital derivations, occurring at the onset of a train of flashes at 20 f.sec.

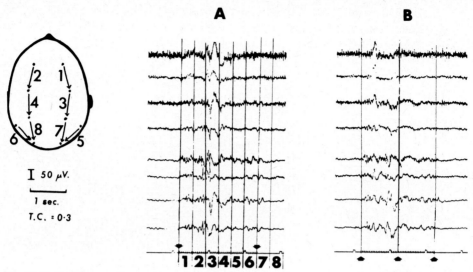

**A**

**B**

I 50 μV.

1 sec.

T.C. = 0·3

1 2 3 4 5 6 7 8

**Fig. 22.** Method of measurement of response to IPS. (A) The two-second train of IPS is divided into 6 equal periods of 1 cm. and the two subsequent centimetres are numbered 7 and 8. A PCR occurs in division 3. (B) Spike and wave confined to the first second (1,2,3) of IPS.

Occasionally a single spike and wave complex occurs at the start of the train of flashes, or after the flashing has ceased. These are 'on' or 'off' responses. They may occur alone or both together (fig. 17). An 'on' response is a modified PCR and is seen through all regions, unlike an exaggerated VEP which is seen only in the occipital regions, but may occur at the start of a train of flashes (fig. 21).

Photoconvulsive responses consisting of spike and wave discharges may occur within the first second of the train of flashes or in the middle of the flash period (fig. 22). In our initial investigation (Jeavons *et al.* 1966) we divided the two-second period of photic stimulation into six divisions of 1 cm. each, numbering them 1-6 and numbering the 2 cms. after the flashing had stopped as 7 and 8 (fig. 22a). This enabled us to measure the moment of onset and the duration of the PCR. In some patients one finds a graded response to each frequency as one approaches the flash rate which consistently evokes a photoconvulsive response of spike and wave. Some samples of PCR in one patient are shown in figure 17, but more commonly the responses are graded according to the flash rate. For example, there might be a slow wave in response to 46 f.sec., an 'on' or 'off' response to 45 f.sec., an 'on' and 'off' response to 44 f.sec., a spike and wave response in periods 1 and 2 at 43 f. sec., and a spike and wave discharge during periods 2 to 7 at 42 f.sec.; if this was confirmed on repeat, then the upper limit would be 42 f.sec.

On the basis of this study we decided to ignore slow waves, single spikes, or spike and wave confined to the first second of photic stimulation (fig. 22b) and to take as the limits any response showing polyspike and wave, or spike and wave persisting after the first second of photic stimulation, unless the discharge was associated with a generalised myoclonic jerk.

For diagnosis of photosensitive epilepsy one only needs to evoke PCR consistently

62

to a number of flash rates. The precise nature or duration of the PCR and the range of flash rates by which it is evoked are not of diagnostic importance though they may be of therapeutic value.

Photoconvulsive responses consisting of 3 c.sec. spike and wave discharges were seen in 401 cases (88 per cent), theta spike and wave in 33 (7 per cent), and other PCR in 15 cases (3 per cent). Spike and wave discharges occurred equally in all groups, but those at 3 c.sec. were commoner in patients with abnormal basic records, while theta spike and wave discharges were commoner in those with normal basic records, and fewer of these patients had photosensitive epilepsy.

In 5 patients no photoconvulsive response was evoked by IPS. One had a history of tonic-clonic seizures precipitated by flickering light. Her basic EEG showed spike and wave discharges after eye closure but no abnormality at all during IPS. This finding was unique and we can give no explanation. One man had a tonic-clonic fit while at work in front of a visual display unit. No abnormality was found either in his basic EEG or on IPS and we did not regard him as suffering from photosensitive epilepsy. Two patients, both with a definite history of fits induced by flickering light, showed only occipital spikes during IPS. One patient who had a fit while adjusting a faulty T.V. picture had a normal basic EEG and no abnormality on IPS on two separate occasions. He is the only case out of 332 photosensitive patients in whom the basic EEG was normal, and we could not confirm photosensitivity in the laboratory.

We therefore consider that for all practical purposes the absence of any abnormality during IPS, *using our techniques,* virtually excludes the diagnosis of photosensitive epilepsy.

*Clinical significance*

In order to obtain some idea of the clinical significance of abnormalities induced by photic stimulation the routine EEG records taken in one EEG department over a period of 10 years (1956-1966) were analysed (Jeavons 1966). All the EEGs had been interpreted by one person and all patients had been exposed to IPS as part of the routine test, although the technique had varied over the years. Abnormality was evoked by IPS in 402 of the 14,141 cases (2.8 per cent). Of the 402, 57 per cent showed 3 c.sec. spike and wave PCR. From this and our subsequent studies, certain tentative conclusions can be drawn.

1. If spike and wave discharges are evoked by IPS the clinical diagnosis is more likely to be epilepsy than a non-epileptic condition, provided the patient does not have a relative with photosensitive epilepsy.
2. Spike and wave discharges evoked by IPS do not necessarily indicate a clinical diagnosis of photosensitive epilepsy.
3. A normal basic EEG with no spike and wave activity either spontaneously or induced by hyperventilation does not differentiate the patient who is clinically photosensitive from the patient who is not photosensitive.
4. Most patients who show spike and wave discharges in the basic EEG following eye closure will have a PCR evoked by IPS and most will have epilepsy. All patients with polyspikes on IPS have epilepsy.
5. If photic stimulation evokes a PCR and generalised myoclonic jerking, it is extremely likely that the patient has epilepsy.

**Clinical responses to IPS**

*Subjective sensations*

Photic stimulation may induce an unpleasant feeling, or a sensation of dizziness, or a sensation of jerking although no jerks are actually observed. In our patients these 'funny' feelings were associated with an abnormal discharge, usually of spike and wave or polyspike and wave, although 3 patients experienced them with occipital spikes. As has already been mentioned, 8 patients noted the same feeling during IPS as they had experienced when exposed to flickering light in an everyday setting. In a few cases the sensation only occurred when a fully developed spike and wave discharge was evoked, but not when a brief 'on' or 'off' response occurred. One patient experienced a different sensation associated with a 3 c.sec. spike and wave PCR to that with a theta spike and wave PCR. One patient reported an unpleasant sensation at certain flash rates which caused her to turn her head away from the lamp. Other flash rates did not evoke this response, yet the EEG recorded from the posterior regions was essentially the same under both conditions. The patient was therefore persuaded to continue to look directly at the centre of the lamp even when the unpleasant sensation was evoked, and when she did this a photoconvulsive response occurred. Thus she was able, after less than a second of photic stimulation, to distinguish a flash rate which would evoke a PCR from one which would not, although the electroencephalographer was unable to do so from observation of the EEG response. One patient who had temporal lobe epilepsy had an epigastric aura with each PCR. Two children obviously enjoyed IPS and one of them was reported to be impulsively attracted to the T.V. screen.

In all, 23 patients experienced peculiar sensations in association with each PCR. We have not, of course, included the many patients who said they disliked IPS, or those who were frightened by it.

*Myoclonic jerks*

In the original survey of photic stimulation (Jeavons 1966), myoclonic jerks evoked by IPS were associated with definite clinical epilepsy in 67 per cent of cases, and with probable epilepsy in 19 per cent. In the present study of 454 patients, myoclonic jerks were evoked by IPS in 97 cases (21 per cent) and were more common in the photosensitive patients (Groups I and II) than in Group III. Sixty-two per cent of those with jerks on IPS have abnormality in their basic record.

Jerking evoked by IPS is significantly related to myoclonic epilepsy ($p. < .001$) and to clinical photosensitivity ($p. < .01$). It is commoner in those who have both spontaneous fits and flicker-induced fits ($p. < .01$), and in the original groups (A-F) there is evidence that the incidence of myoclonic jerks on IPS and the incidence of myoclonic epilepsy are correlated ($p. < .05$), using rank orders in which a score of one indicates highest incidence.

|  | *Groups* | | | | | |
|---|---|---|---|---|---|---|
| Myoclonic jerks on IPS | D | E | A | B | F | C |
| Clinical myoclonic epilepsy | D | E | B | F | A | C |
| Rank order | 1 | 2 | 3 | 4 | 5 | 6 |

64

*Fits*

Thirty-six patients had some type of seizure under photic stimulation.

Three patients had a tonic-clonic seizure. The first fit occurred long before we had developed our present technique and was entirely due to the technician continuing photic stimulation for about 10 seconds after the appearance of spike and wave discharge. The second patient had been investigated on two previous occasions and her sensitivity limits had been established. We were attempting 'conditioning' or extinction using the method described by Forster and Campos (1964) with a large back-illuminated screen with the photostimulator in the centre. Paroxysmal theta activity appeared after only a second of photic stimulation, and a tonic-clonic seizure then occurred (see p. 97-8). We attributed this to the extinction technique, but on subsequent routine testing with IPS the patient again developed a tonic-clonic fit. On both these occasions the testing was done in the pre-menstrual week, whereas the much longer IPS sessions which had not evoked a fit had taken place at different points in her cycle, and it appears likely that her sensitivity to flicker was markedly influenced by her hormonal levels. The third patient, a boy with myoclonic astatic epilepsy and subnormality, had no abnormality on IPS at the age of 14 months, but on re-testing at the age of 2 years IPS evoked a tonic-clonic fit, and the same occurred at the age of 3 years. On both occasions the fit occurred immediately on exposure to flicker. He subsequently received sodium valproate and re-testing showed photoconvulsive responses to IPS between 10 and 17 f.sec. with associated myoclonic jerks, but no fit occurred.

In two other patients IPS evoked long psychomotor attacks with automatisms, the fit lasting several minutes.

The commonest seizure to be evoked is an absence, with associated 3 c.sec. spike and wave discharges, some being typical and lasting 5-15 seconds, others being atypical and lasting up to 50 seconds. In the longer attacks, although the patient often does not respond during the first 5-10 seconds, some response may be obtained later in the attack, though these responses may not be normal. For example, one child would not respond at all during the first ten seconds, would then answer questions incorrectly, and would finally give the correct answer to a simple sum, whereupon the discharge ceased having lasted 40-50 seconds. It is a common finding that the discharge may terminate and the attack cease in response to an auditory stimulus (whistle, hand-clap, or calling the patient's name). It is also characteristic of these patients that the invariable response to IPS is a discharge of 3 c.sec. spike and wave, and that this response can only be obtained over a narrow range of flash rates (fig. 23). In fact, 22 of 29 such patients tested for sensitivity limits showed a range of less than 14 flash rates. Twenty-five were more sensitive with eyes open than with eyes closed.

This relatively small group of 31 patients in whom an absence is induced shows a higher proportion of females (77 per cent) than either the individual groups (A-F) or the whole series. The mean age is 12 years. Spontaneous spike and wave discharges occurred in the basic EEGs of 20 (65 per cent), and nearly half (45 per cent) did not have clinical photosensitivity. Typical or atypical absences occurred spontaneously in 27 patients (55 per cent) and in 10 of them were the only type of fit experienced. Two

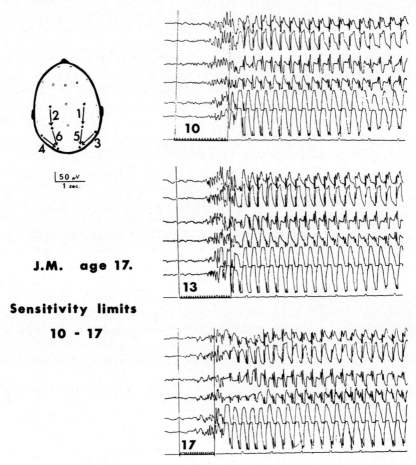

J.M. age 17.

Sensitivity limits

10 - 17

**Fig. 23.** 3 c.sec. spike and wave with typical absence induced by a narrow range of flash rates (10-17 f.sec. only).

patients were impulsively attracted to the T.V. screen.

Thus the characteristic patient of this small group is a girl aged 12 who has absences, who shows spike and wave discharges in her basic record, and in whom IPS, over a narrow range of frequencies, induces a 3 c.sec. spike and wave discharge with an associated absence usually lasting from 5-15 seconds. The treatment of choice is sodium valproate (Jeavons and Clark 1974).

**Sensitivity limits**

The sensitivity limit is defined as the highest or lowest flash rate which consistently evokes a spike and wave or polyspike and wave photoconvulsive response (p. 58). The lower limit is usually more easily defined than the upper, owing to the tendency of photostimulators to produce subharmonic components at fast flash rates. The sensitivity range (SR) is obtained by subtracting the lower

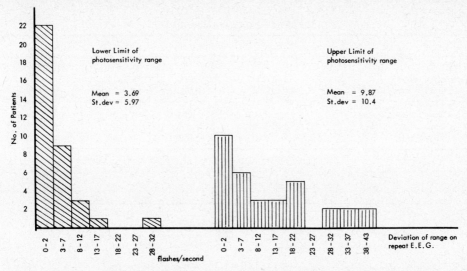

**Fig. 24.** Deviation in the eyes-open sensitivity limits for a combined sample of 36 male and female patients repeated within a 3 month period (age range 7-30). The lower limit (on the left) shows greater repeatability than the upper limit (right).

limit from the upper limit, thus indicating the number of flash rates to which the patient is sensitive. For example, a patient who shows a PCR in response to 12 f.sec. but not to 11 f.sec. and to 54 f.sec. but not 55 f.sec., has a lower limit of 12, an upper limit of 54, and a sensitivity range of 42.

It was not always possible to establish the sensitivity limits, usually because of inconstant responses. In a few cases the patient was apprehensive and would not look at the lamp. In the first 157 patients we tested, it was not possible to assess the limits in 18 cases (11.5 per cent). It became apparent that the inconstancy of the responses was sometimes due to shifting of the patient's gaze, and on testing the effect of direction of gaze we found that unless the patient looked directly at the centre of the lamp a PCR might not be evoked. In the subsequent 131 patients whose sensitivity limits were tested, inconstant responses were only found in 6 cases (4.6 per cent), and there is little doubt that the reason for this reduction in 'failed' tests has been our insistence that the patient looks at the centre of the lamp throughout IPS (see page 75).

We investigated the long term test-retest reliability of upper and lower sensitivity limits on 36 patients whose EEGs were repeated within a three-month period. All the patients were drug-free on both occasions, and the age range was between 7 and 30 years.

The reliability of the lower limit was found to be much greater than the upper (fig. 24). Twenty-two of the 36 patients showed a difference of 2 f.sec. or less between their lower limits on the second EEG and the original test. The upper limit showed much more deviation in many patients, and only 10 patients had 2 f.sec. or less difference in their upper limit on the two tests. The mean deviation

67

## TABLE IX
### Sensitivity according to state of eyes

|  | Group I | Group II | Group III | All cases |
|---|---|---|---|---|
| Total tested | 125 | 84 | 83 | 292 |
| Eyes open only | 71 (57%) | 49 (58%) | 56 (67%) | 176 (60%) |
| Eyes open > eyes closed | 44 (35%) | 27 (32%) | 11 (13%) | 82 (28%) |
| Eyes closed only | 3 ( 2%) | — | 2 ( 2%) | 5 ( 2%) |
| Eyes closed > eyes open | 1 (0.8%) | 5 ( 6%) | 8 (10%) | 14 ( 5%) |
| Eyes open = eyes closed | 2 (1.6%) | 1 (1.2%) | 3 ( 4%) | 6 ( 2%) |
| Eye closure only | 4 (32%) | 2 (2.4%) | 3 ( 4%) | 9 ( 3%) |

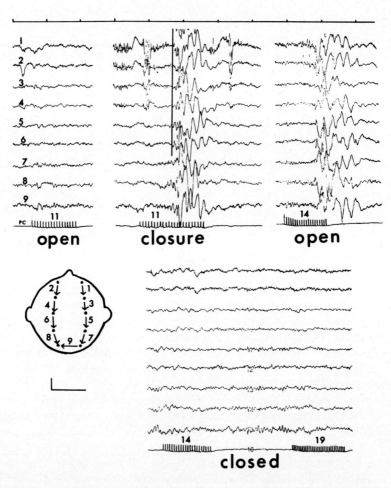

**Fig. 25.** Comparison of response to IPS in different states of the eyes. 11 f.sec. evokes PCR only on eye closure, whereas 14 f.sec. evokes PCR with eyes left open. Neither 14 or 19 f.sec. evokes abnormality when eyes are kept closed. Calibration 100 μv and 1 second. (From Panayiotopoulos 1974.)

68

for the lower limit was 3.69 f.sec. (standard deviation 5.97), and for the upper limit 9.87 f.sec. (standard deviation 10.4).

We had often suspected that the upper limit was more variable and it is possible that this finding reflects the unreliability of photostimulators at high flash rates. For example, subharmonic modulations of a 70 f.sec. stimulus can produce a false positive response when the true upper limit is only 35 f.sec.

We were able to establish the sensitivity limits in 292 cases. Using the sensitivity range as our criterion we divided the cases according to whether the sensitivity was greater with eyes open or eyes closed. Table IX clearly shows that most patients are more sensitive with eyes open (88 per cent) and that 60 per cent are sensitive *only* when their eyes are open.

It is logical to expect less sensitivity with eyes closed than with eyes open, and when the eyes are closed it is more difficult to establish the limits with any accuracy. Closing the eyes reduces the intensity of the flicker stimulus by interposing a red diffusion filter which also reduces pattern. Furthermore, the eyes are no longer centrally fixated on the lamp, causing further reduction in the number of cells stimulated (see page 108). In a few cases we have been able to induc a PCR at a flash rate not previously effective with eyes closed, by asking the patient to imagine looking at the centre of the lamp and to move his or her eyes to that point.

Of the 292 cases 9 patients (3 per cent) showed no abnormality in either the eyes open or eyes closed condition but did demonstrate a PCR following the act of eye closure during IPS. We re-iterate that in our investigations patients are stimulated either with the eyes kept open or kept closed. It is only when no abnormality is provoked by either of these two conditions that the act of eye closure during IPS is investigated (fig. 12), since this is the most provocative condition. Comparative responses to IPS under the three conditions are shown in Figure 25, which illustrates that a PCR may be evoked by IPS at 11 f.sec. following eye closure, when it cannot be obtained until 14 f.sec. with eyes open, and is never obtained with the eyes kept closed.

## Clinical importance of sensitivity limits and sensitivity range

On the basis of the modal sensitivity range we divided 157 cases into those with a wide range, SR > 34, and those with a narrow range, SR < 34. For statistical comparison we compared 42 cases with an SR of 1-14 with 41 with an SR of 52-80. The only significant finding (p. < .001) was that wide ranges were more common in Group I than Groups II and III. The width of sensitivity range was not related to close T.V. viewing. Wide ranges were more common in those who were more sensitive with eyes open than closed. Thus the actual sensitivity range does not appear to have clinical significance.

Sensitivity limits and the actual frequencies to which the individual is sensitive are however important from the point of view of diagnosis and therapy.

Figure 26 shows the individual sensitivity ranges with eyes open and eyes closed in 52 patients. Figure 27 is based on 170 patients in whom sensitivity limits could be established with accuracy, and shows the percentage of patients sensitive to each of the flash rates.

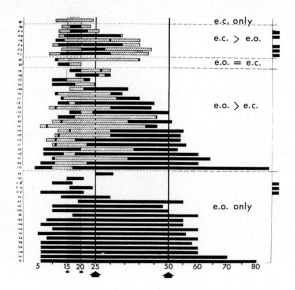

Fig. 26. Comparison of sensitivity ranges in 52 patients. Solid lines indicate sensitivity range with eyes open and cross-hatched lines the range with eyes closed. The short black bars on the right indicate the 8 patients who did not have television epilepsy.

SENSITIVITY TO INDIVIDUAL FLASH RATES

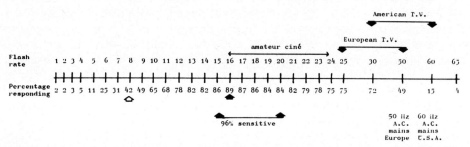

Fig. 27. The percentage of patients (N = 170) producing a PCR in response to each flash rate. The open arrow shows that 42 per cent of patients were sensitive to 8 f.sec. (see text). 96 per cent of patients were sensitive to flash rates between 15 and 20 f.sec., and 89 per cent showed a PCR in response to 16 f.sec. Examples of the flicker rate of environmental stimuli are shown above (amateur cine, European and American T.V.).

Four patients have shown a spike and wave complex in response to a single flash and in two of them we have confirmed, by using a computer of average transients (CAT), that the response is a true spike and wave and not an exaggerated visual evoked potential.

Three patients showed a PCR only in response to a single flash rate (10 f.sec., 16 f.sec. and 18 f.sec.). In one of these patients, a girl aged 7 years, 10 f.sec. evoked a 65 second discharge of 2 c.sec. spike and wave activity on two separate occasions. During the discharges the child responded to questioning. Two patients have shown a PCR to two separate flash rates—in one case at 10 and 20 f.sec., and in the other to 13 and 18 f.sec. Several patients have very narrow sensitivity ranges (2 to 4 flash rates).

It can be seen from Figure 27 that 89 per cent of cases will show a photoconvulsive response to 16 f.sec. and that if one tests all flash rates between 15 and 20 per second a PCR will be produced in 96 per cent of patients.

Amateur cine projectors flicker at rates between 16 and 24 per second so many photosensitive patients are at risk when watching home movies, though fits under these circumstances are in fact rare, probably because home cine equipment is not common.

In 1971 the Greater London Council forbade the use of flicker rates faster than 8 per second in discotheques. Although this ban reduces the risk to those who frequent discotheques (it should be remembered that the population at greatest risk from photosensitivity is female, aged 9 to 14 years), 42 per cent of our patients were still sensitive to 8 f.sec., 31 per cent to 7 f.sec., and one quarter to 6 f.sec., so such an edict, to be really effective, would have to ban flash rates above 5 per second.

'Television' epilepsy is more common in Europe, where the frequency of the a.c. mains is 50 Hz., than in the U.S.A., where it is 60 Hz. In British television there are two principal flicker frequencies—50 Hz. and 25 Hz. "If a large plain area of the televised scene is viewed at (say) four times picture height, only 50 Hz. flicker is present. The 25 Hz. component arises from interference effects (Moiré patterns) produced by televising a pattern of horizontal or near-horizontal lines. If the spacing of the lines in the pattern is similar to spacing between the lines of the television picture a coarse pattern is produced which flickers at 25 Hz. This is much more obvious flicker than the 50 Hz., which is present all the time. The brightness level varies with the age of the set and the personal choice of the viewer, the usual brightness level of white being about 20-25 foot-Lamberts (ft-L), though modern television tubes can easily give 50 ft-L. The range is probably 10-35 ft-L. The 50 Hz. flicker tends to become very objectionable if the brightness is set to the highest level. The 50 Hz. component of the flicker is not influenced by the number of lines (405 or 625). The 25 Hz. component is dependent on the production of Moiré effects and although in theory these should be equally likely for each of the two line standards, in fact they are more severe on the 405-line standard because of the limited resolving power of television cameras and film scanners" (Gouriet, personal communication 1966).

Table X shows the percentage of patients with 'television' epilepsy who are sensitive to the main T.V. flicker rates in Europe and the U.S.A. Although the highest proportion of patients are sensitive to 25 f.sec., almost as many are sensitive to 30 f.sec. and 61 per cent are sensitive to 50 f.sec. (fig. 28). Abnormality was evoked by flash rates of 25 and 50 per second in 60 per cent of all 116 patients, whilst only 22 per cent were sensitive to 30 and 60 f.sec. It is of interest that those patients who have not had a fit induced by television tend to be more sensitive to IPS with eyes closed than with eyes open (fig. 26) or to have narrow sensitivity ranges at low flash rates (less than 25 f.sec.). A few patients with 'television' epilepsy did not show abnormality on IPS at flash rates of 25 per second and above. Thus it would seem that the main reason for epilepsy being less commonly associated with television viewing in the U.S.A. is the higher flicker rate of 60 Hz. We have no evidence as to the effect of 405 or 625 lines, or of colour versus black and white. In one or two cases fits have occurred when the family purchased a set with a larger screen.

71

## TABLE X
### Sensitivity and flash rates related to T.V.-induced fits

| Flash rates | Number sensitive | % |
|:---:|:---:|:---:|
| 25 | 99 | 85 |
| 30 | 92 | 79 |
| 50 | 71 | 61 |
| 60 | 25 | 22 |
| | | |
| 25 + 50 | 70 | 60 |
| 30 + 60 | 25 | 22 |
| *Total patients* | 116 | 100 |

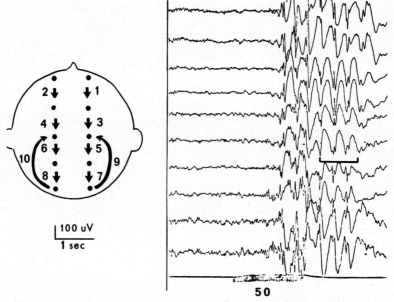

**Fig. 28.** A photoconvulsive response of 3 c.sec. spike and wave evoked by flicker at the fundamental T.V. rate (50 f.sec.).

## Analysis of basic EEG

In 8 patients frequency analysis of the spontaneous EEG was carried out using a BNI low-frequency wave analyser. The analyser had been modified to provide an automated output suitable for computation (Bailey and Harding 1966). Analysis was made of the alpha activity in the resting state, both with eyes open and with eyes closed. Computations were made of the harmonic mean frequency and variability (Kendalls W) in both these conditions and the findings compared to the patients' sensitivity ranges with eyes open and closed. There was no relationship between the harmonic mean frequency and the mean of the sensitivity range in either condition, or between the variability score and the width of the sensitivity range.

72

# CHAPTER 7

# Laboratory Studies: Factors affecting Photosensitivity

## Introduction

The studies in the last chapter have been concerned with developing a standardised technique for intermittent photic stimulation and with the associated EEG and behavioural responses. Following the establishment of these diagnostic criteria we felt that further studies were required of factors which may influence the patient's response to photic stimulation, such as whether one or both eyes are stimulated, the direction of gaze and the angle of illumination, the use of a coloured stimulus and the presence of pattern. We felt that further investigation of the EEG responses to photic stimulation was necessary and that we should try to elucidate the contribution made by abnormal responses of the visual cortex.

## Monocular stimulation

The effect of monocular stimulation was tested in 244 patients. In 164 (67 per cent) no abnormality occurred (fig. 15), and in 75 cases there was less abnormality than with binocular stimulation. Only in 5 cases was there no inhibition of abnormality when one eye was covered. There was no difference in the monocular response in relation to the presence or absence of spontaneous spike and wave abnormalities in the basic record, nor was there any relation with the clinical group.

Our early method of testing the effect of monocular stimulation was to cover one of the patient's eyes with a pad of cottonwool on top of which was placed a light-proof patch. Using this method we established the sensitivity limits and compared the sensitivity ranges on monocular stimulation with those on binocular stimulation (fig. 29) in 17 patients. Patients numbered 1-8 had normal basic EEGs and patients 9-17 showed 'spontaneous' spike and wave discharges in their basic records. In 10 patients there was still some abnormality on monocular stimulation, but in all cases the sensitivity ranges were narrower. In 7 of these 10 abnormality occurred on monocular stimulation of either eye. The 9 patients with spike and wave discharges in their basic records showed greater sensitivity to monocular stimulation, more polyspike and wave discharges on IPS, and more myoclonic jerks during IPS than the 8 patients who had normal basic EEGs. Although there is clear evidence that patients are less sensitive on monocular stimulation the overall pattern of sensitivity remains the same. The number of patients sensitive to each flash rate is reduced, but the peak of sensitivity remains between 16 and 20 f.sec. (fig. 30). It should be noted that the method used in this investigation was different from that used in the 244 patients mentioned above; with the later method only one or two flash rates were tested and there was no apparent difference in relation to spontaneous abnormalities.

Subsequently we changed the method of monocular stimulation and asked the patient to press the palm of the hand firmly over the orbit, making sure that the hand was closely applied to the edge of the nose (fig. 31). We did not test a range of

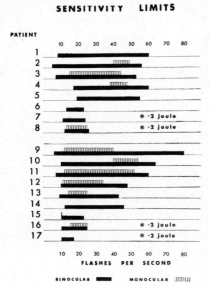

SENSITIVITY LIMITS

PATIENT

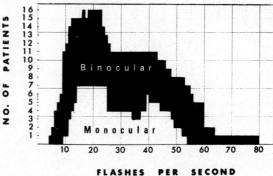

FLASHES PER SECOND

**Fig. 30.** Comparison of binocular and monocular stimulation in 16 patients. Peak sensitivity is at 20 f.sec. in both states and the pattern of sensitivity is similar, but the monocular responses are markedly reduced.

**Fig. 29.** Comparison of sensitivity limits in 17 patients, with binocular and monocular stimulation. Patients 1-8 have normal basic EEGs, and 9-17 have spontaneous spike and wave discharges. Patients 1, 5, 6, 7, 14 and 17 do not have a PCR on monocular stimulation at any flash rate. Patient 15 is sensitive on monocular stimulation to 10 f.sec. only.

**Fig. 31**(right). Monocular stimulation with subject covering one eye. The palm of the hand is pressed firmly into the orbit with the lateral edge up against the nose.

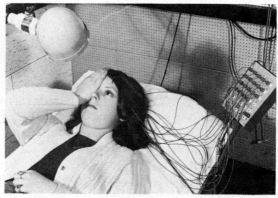

frequencies, but tested each eye at a flash rate just above the patient's lower limit. In a few cases we tested at 25 or 50 f.sec. The selected stimulus was first given with both eyes open and, provided that a PCR was evoked, one eye was covered and the same stimulus given on three occasions to each eye, usually for a period of 5-10 seconds. It was quite common to find that there was no abnormality when the first eye was tested (whether it was right or left), but the initial testing of the second eye was associated with a PCR. If the patient was encouraged to press the hand firmly into the orbit the abnormality did not usually appear with subsequent testing. However, some patients did show different responses from the two eyes. In 56 patients there was less abnormality on monocular stimulation than on binocular stimulation, but responses were still evoked and we were able to compare the effect of stimulation to the right and left eyes. In 27 of the 56, inhibition was equal whichever eye was stimulated, in 15 inhibition was greater when the left eye was covered, and in 14 when the right eye was

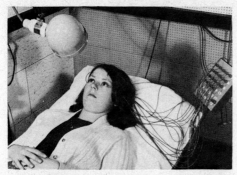

**Fig. 32.** Subject looking at centre of lamp, which is 30 cm. from the eyes. Eyes and face clearly visible to the technician.

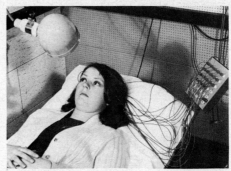

**Fig. 33.** Subject looking at right hand edge of lamp. Compare with Figure 32.

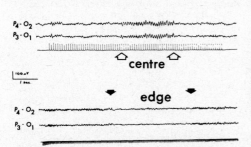

**Fig. 34.** Effect on the EEG of patient looking at centre and edge of lamp. Only when the patient looks at the centre are occipital spikes evoked by 12 f.sec. (upper traces). Photic driving is only evoked by 24 f.sec. when the patient is looking at the centre of the lamp, and ceases when she looks at the edge.

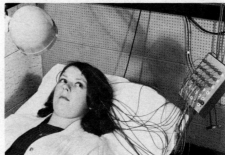

**Fig. 35.** Lateral gaze. Subject looking as far to the left as possible.

covered. In most cases there was no definite history of impaired vision, but in two patients inhibition occurred only when the eye with impaired visual acuity was stimulated, confirming the findings of Parsons-Smith (1953)

**Direction of gaze and angle of illumination**

Preliminary testing indicated that if the patient did not look at the centre of the lamp a PCR might not be evoked (see p. 67)

We therefore drew an open circle of 2.5 cm. diameter in the centre of the glass of the lamp and placed a coloured marker on the outer rim of the lamp. The patient was asked to stare either into the small circle (fig. 32) or to look at the marker on the edge (fig. 33). According to whether the Grass or Kaiser lamp was used, the shift of gaze was 12° or 15°. Of the 18 patients tested in this manner, PCR responses were inhibited or reduced in 9 patients, but in the other 9 the slight change in direction of

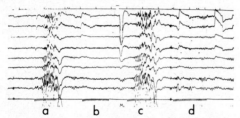

**Fig. 36.** Effect of direction of gaze on EEG response to IPS. (Standard parasagittal montage. Gain 100 μv/cm. Paper speed 3 cm/sec.) (a) Gaze forwards, (b) Gaze upwards, (c) Gaze forwards, (d) Gaze downwards.

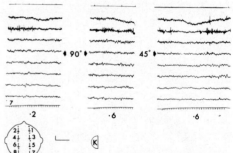

**Fig. 37.** Effect of lateral illumination using Kaiser photostimulator. The left-hand trace shows no abnormality evoked by stimulation at 7 f.sec. with photostimulator at 90° to forward gaze (intensity 0.2 joules). The middle trace shows no abnormality even with increased intensity. The right hand trace shows no abnormality at maximum intensity and the lamp at 45°. (Same patient as Figure 15). Calibration 100 μv and 1 second.

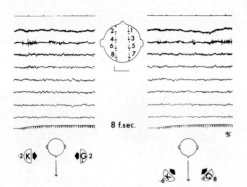

**Fig. 38.** Same patient as Figure 37. Shows effect of stimulation with two lamps. The patient is looking forward at all times. K = Kaiser; G = Grass with grid. Intensity of each lamp is shown. It should be noted that although both stimulators are set at 8 f.sec., they are not in phase. Calibration 100 μv and 1 second. (From Jeavons *et al.* 1971.).

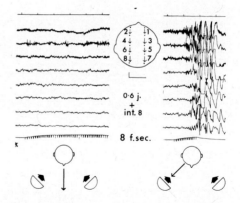

**Fig. 39.** Same patient as Figures 37 and 38. A PCR is evoked when the patient looks at one of the lamps (right hand trace).

gaze did not have an obvious effect in reducing the PCRs. We also tested the effect on photic driving in non-epileptic patients and found that this also was reduced when the patient looked at the edge of the lamp (fig. 34).

We then tested the effect of lateral gaze, asking the patient to keep his head in a central position in front of the lamp, but to turn his gaze as far as possible to one side (fig. 35). Of 91 patients tested in this way no PCR could be evoked in 89, even when the intensity of the light was increased. A single patient showed a PCR when looking to right or left and a further patient showed a PCR when gazing to the right but not to the left. In a few cases we tested the effect of upwards or downwards gaze with similar results (fig. 36).

Since a change in direction of gaze had such a marked effect (much greater than the inhibition with monocular stimulation) we tested the effect of lateral illumination by placing the lamp at 90° from forward gaze and found that no abnormality was evoked by IPS. We then placed the lamp at 45° and still found no abnormality (fig. 37). At an angle of 90° the nose prevents the flicker stimulus from reaching the farther eye, so that the situation is similar to monocular stimulation. We therefore placed a lamp on each side of the patient's head, switched them on simultaneously at approximately the same rate, and found no abnormality could be induced when the lamps were at 90° or even at 45° (fig. 38). If the patient was asked to keep his head still, but gaze at one of the lamps at the side, a PCR was evoked (fig. 39).

We have subsequently tested, as part of our routine investigation of all photosensitive patients, the effect of one lamp placed at 30° to the side of forward gaze, the patient being asked to stare at a mark on the wall straight ahead. We test at Grass intensity 1, 2, 4 and 8 and have also used intensity 16 in some cases. The duration of the stimulus always exceeds 5 seconds and usually lasts 10 seconds. We have tested 52 patients and *none* have shown a PCR when illuminated from an angle at intensities 1, 2 and 4. We do not routinely use intensity 8, but none of the patients tested has shown abnormality at this intensity. Intensity 16 cannot be used for long periods since at this degree of brightness the photostimulator has a self-limiting device which switches off to prevent accidental prolonged exposure.

**Pattern**

During EEG investigation of the photosensitive patients, we noted that flash frequencies which induced occipital spikes or photoconvulsive responses when using the Kaiser photostimulator were less effective, or not effective, when using a Grass photostimulator. Although various factors can alter the efficiency of photic stimulation (see above) and although there were many differences between the stroboscopes, the most obvious difference was the presence in the Kaiser stroboscope of a metal grid. This grid is placed between the gas discharge tube and the glass as a protection against accidental explosion of the tube. When the tube is illuminated the grid appears to the patient as a pattern of squares.

In a pilot study of 4 patients, IPS at 0.1 joule from the Kaiser photostimulator consistently evoked EEG abnormalities. No abnormalities were evoked by the Grass photostimulator, even at its highest intensity (intensity 16). However, when the Kaiser metal grid was fitted to the Grass photostimulator, even intensity 2 would consistently evoke abnormalities (fig. 40). We therefore studied the effectiveness of various patterns combined with IPS in evoking either photoconvulsive responses or occipital spikes.

We investigated 10 consecutive patients with epilepsy who showed EEG abnormalities during IPS (page 4). Seven had fits precipitated by television viewing (Group I) and in 3 there was no clinical history of photosensitive epilepsy (Group III).

The lamp of the photostimulator was placed at the normal distance of 30 cm. directly in front of the patient's eyes, and the patient was instructed to look at the centre of the lamp. Each burst of IPS was given for approximately two seconds, but was discontinued as soon as a PCR occurred.

77

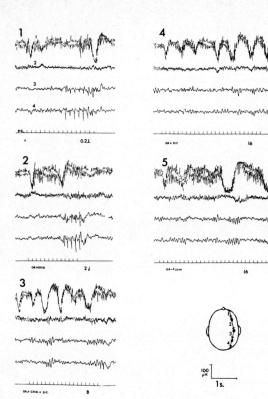

**Fig. 40.** Pilot study comparing Kaiser and Grass photostimulators. (1) Kaiser (0.2 joules) 6 f.sec. evokes occipital spikes; (2) Grass (intensity 2) fitted with Kaiser grid evokes similar response; (3) Grass (intensity 8) with diffuser in front of grid only evokes slight abnormality; (4) Grass (intensity 16), with diffuser only, does not evoke abnormality; (5) Grass with plain glass (as supplied by manufacturers) does not evoke abnormality at maximum intensity (16). (From Panayiotopoulos 1972.)

## TABLE XI
### Intensities of Kaiser and Grass photostimulators

|  | Mean luminance at 20 f.sec. Nits (candellas/sq. metre) | Stimulus intensity of one pulse in nit seconds |
|---|---|---|
| Kaiser intensity | | |
| 0.1 joules | 431 | 22 |
| 0.2 joules | 2161 | 108 |
| Grass intensity | | |
| 1 | 1058 | 53 |
| 2 | 1363 | 68 |
| 4 | 1925 | 96 |
| 8 | 3939 | 197 |
| 16 | 9661 | 483 |

Although clinical observation suggested that it was the pattern of the grid which was the important factor in differentiating the effectiveness of the two photostimulators, it was obviously important also to compare the other properties of the lamps. Unfortunately the manufacturers of the photostimulators do not provide suitable data on intensity of luminance for comparison, and several methods were tried before it was decided to use an S.E.I. photometer.

78

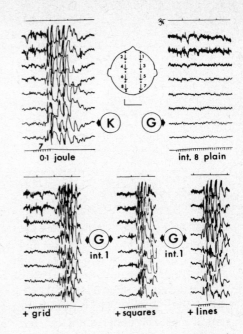

**Fig. 41.** Patterns used with Grass lamp. Upper left: Kaiser metal grid. Upper right: fine grid (dry print transfer). Lower left: fine lines, used vertically and horizontally (dry print transfer). Lower right: heavy grid (dry print transfer).

**Fig. 42** (right). Effect, in one patient, of patterns shown in Figure 41 compared to effect of Kaiser photostimulator (K). Upper right hand trace shows response to Grass at increased intensity with no pattern. (From Jeavons *et al.* 1972).

A photic stimulus is best characterised by the spatial and temporal distribution of luminance in the visual field. The spectral composition of the light can be significant, but in the present investigation the comparison involved two instruments using Xenon tubes giving white light of essentially similar composition.

The mean luminance of the stimulators, viewed from the normal distance of operation (30 cm.) at a frequency of 20 f.sec. at various intensities, was measured with the photometer and the results obtained in foot lamberts were converted to candellas per square metre, or nits. The effective stimulus of each pulse was then deduced in terms of nit seconds by dividing the mean luminance by the number of pulses. A discussion of the value of this method will be found in the Appendix. Table XI shows the intensities of the two photostimulators.

The two light sources presented slightly different circular patches of light, the Kaiser subtending a visual angle of 28° and the Grass 24.4° when viewed at 30 cm. It was noticed, however, that the luminance in the periphery of the larger stimulator fell off more rapidly owing to the use of a less efficient diffuser, and in view of the high representation of the central area of the visual field in the cortex it was felt that the differences could be neglected.

Since the pilot study had shown that the effectiveness of the Grass photo-stimulator could be altered by adding the Kaiser grid, further simple patterns and a diffuser were made for the Grass lamp:

(1) A pattern of small squares with narrow (0.3 mm.) black lines set at the same aperture spacing (2 mm. × 2 mm.) as the Kaiser grid. The squares thus produced subtended a visual angle of 22′.

## TABLE XII
### Effect of patterned stimulus in 10 patients

| | Grass intensity | | | | |
| | 1 | 2 | 4 | 8 | 16 |
|---|---|---|---|---|---|
| Diffuser | — | 2 | — | — | — |
| Plain glass | — | — | 1 | 2 | — |
| Large squares | 1 | — | — | 5 | 3 |
| Horizontal lines | 5 | 2 | 2 | — | 1 |
| Vertical lines | 6 | 3 | 1 | | |
| Metal grid | 9 | — | — | — | 1 |
| Small squares | 10 | — | — | — | — |

The figures indicate the number of patients showing a photoconvulsive response to the test frequency.

(2) Vertical thin (1 mm.) black lines subtending 11′, spaced 1.5 mm. apart (17′). This pattern was also rotated and used for the horizontal configuration.

(3) Large squares with thick (3 mm.) black lines subtending 34′ forming 3 mm. × 3 mm. apertures subtending 34′ of arc.

All the above patterns (fig. 41) were on a slightly opaque background which had some diffusing effect. The various patterns, or the grid, were placed behind the plain glass of the Grass photostimulator, but when the diffuser was used it was substituted for the glass. The metal of the Kaiser grid tended to reflect a little light. Care was taken to fit the patterns in a true vertical or horizontal meridian, as previous studies (Bickford and Klass 1969) had shown that increasing the angle from the vertical reduced the effectiveness of pattern.

For each patient we established a flash rate which constantly evoked a photoconvulsive response, using the Kaiser photostimulator at 0.1 J, and used this flash rate as a standard test frequency with the Grass photostimulator.

Testing was carried out under the following IPS conditions presented in random order: (a) diffuser; (b) plain glass; (c) large squares; (d) horizontal lines; (e) vertical lines; (f) metal grid; (g) small squares. If no abnormality was provoked at intensity 1 of the Grass stimulator, further testing was carried out using intensities 2, 4, 8, 16 until abnormality occurred or maximal intensity was reached. The responses of one patient to these various conditions are shown in Figure 42.

The responses of the 10 patients to the 7 IPS conditions are shown in Table XII. When the Grass photostimulator was used at intensity 1, no patient showed a PCR with the diffuser or plain glass and only one showed a PCR when the 'large squares' were used. Horizontal and vertical lines, however, induced a spike and wave discharge in 5 and 6 patients respectively. Nine patients showed a PCR when the Kaiser metal grid was added to the Grass lamp. The small squares were the most effective, provoking a PCR in all 10 patients.

From these findings it is clear that IPS has a greater provocative effect in eliciting EEG abnormalities when it is combined with geometric patterns. The most effective pattern was of small squares formed by narrow lines, and next were parallel lines closely spaced. Squares formed by thick lines were less effective, probably because of reduction in light transmission. Although the luminance of the Kaiser photostimulator set at 0.1 J was less than the lowest value for the Grass stimulator, the latter was relatively ineffective without the addition of some pattern.

These findings are similar to those of Bickford and Klass (1962) and Chatrian *et al.* (1970), both of whom were mainly concerned with straightforward pattern presentation. Some of their patients had clinical pattern-sensitive epilepsy and all of them showed EEG abnormalities during simple pattern presentation. The similarities between our results and those of the above authors suggest that pattern-sensitive and photosensitive epilepsy are closely related. The mechanism whereby the pattern enhances the efficiency of IPS in photosensitive epilepsy may be similar to that in pattern-sensitive epilepsy, the difference being that flickering light is more potent in photosensitive epilepsy than patterns alone, while patterns have a greate. provocative effect than flickering light in pattern-sensitive epilepsy.

There is further similarity between our results and those of authors who investigated the effect of pattern on visual evoked potentials (VEP). Although most of these authors have used pattern reversal as the stimulus—either black and white bars (Gross *et al.* 1967) or chequer board patterns (Spekreijse 1966, Cobb *et al.* 1967, Harter and White 1970)—some have investigated evoked potentials to patterns superimposed on light flashes (Spehlmann 1965, Harter and Salmon 1971). There is some agreement between authors that the optimum square size for eliciting evoked potentials falls within the range 10-20′ visual angle (Spekreijse 1966, van der Tweel and Spekreijse 1968, Harter and White 1970). In our study the most effective pattern (small squares) for producing a PCR had squares which subtended 22′ of visual angle. That the superimposition of structured pattern on to light flashes produces such marked enhancement of cortical response is hardly surprising, since the work of Hubel and Wiesel (1962, 1965, 1968) demonstrates that many cortical neurones respond only to contrast and contour, and not to diffuse light.

A recent study by Engel (1974) has compared the efficacy of diffuse and patterned flash in provoking photoconvulsive responses. A Devices type 3180 photo-stimulator incorporating a transluscent screen was used, and the pattern was produced by superimposing on this a chequer-board of alternate black and white squares of 20′ visual angle. Twenty-eight patients who showed consistent photoconvulsive responses were investigated. Seven of these patients were sensitive to diffuse flash alone; 16 were sensitive to both diffuse and patterned flash, and 5 were only sensitive to patterned flash. It appears to us probable that the difference in results between this study and those we have obtained is due to the type of pattern used. The addition of the chequer-board pattern with its alternate solid black squares would markedly reduce the intensity of the stimulus, and Engel's findings are similar to the findings we obtained with the thick grid line pattern (3 mm. lines, 3 mm. apertures), which was not an effective stimulus because it reduced the intensity of the lamp. It is unfortunate that Engel did not compensate for the intensity factor. Our pattern of fine grid lines obviously has less effect on intensity than blacking out approximately half the lamp.

Since it is apparent that patterns combined with IPS markedly increase the probability of evoking abnormal responses in patients with photosensitive epilepsy there is no doubt that photostimulators without a metal grid should be fitted with a

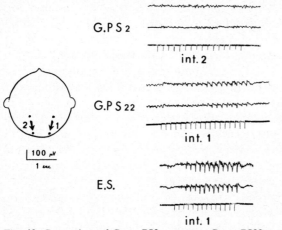

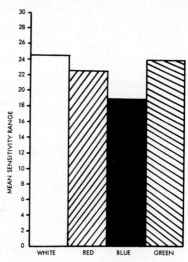

**Fig. 43.** Comparison of Grass PS2, new type Grass PS22, and Elema Schönander photostimulators. The greatest abnormality is evoked by the Elema Schönander, the least by the obsolete Grass PS2.

**Fig. 44.** Histogram showing the mean sensitivity range for 16 patients, using 4 colours. Blue light is the least provocative, and there is no significant difference between the other 3 colours.

pattern of small squares for routine clinical use.

We have recently used a photostimulator made by Elema Schönander. Although we have not yet studied this photostimulator systematically we have found in clinical use that its efficacy, when fitted with a squared pattern, is greater than either the Grass PS2 or PS22 or the Kaiser. The Grass PS22 has a faceted diffusing glass which obscures any pattern placed behind it. We therefore placed a Kaiser metal grid in front of it and compared the effects of this modified photostimulator with the effects of the Grass PS2 with grid behind a diffuser and with the Elema Schönander with added squares pattern (fig. 43). The combination of the faceted glass and the external grid resulted in the PS22 evoking abnormality when none occurred with the PS2 with internal grid, but the Elema Schönander was certainly the most potent, probably because of the larger diameter of the lamp and resultant larger area of retinal stimulation.

We have noted that the use of the squared pattern with a photostimulator may increase the percentage of the 'normal' population who show photoconvulsive responses. Although we have not systematically studied a large normal population, at least three individuals, all female, who have no personal or familial history of epilepsy, have shown photoconvulsive responses to IPS with pattern. Whether this is a danger of the device or simply an improvement of its diagnostic efficiency is a matter of opinion. A photoconvulsive response is evidence of sensitivity to intermittent photic stimulation and is not evidence of photosensitive epilepsy. Such an individual is at risk with flickering lights but the level of risk may be low, and he or she has presumably never been faced with a visual stimulus in the world outside the laboratory sufficiently provocative to cause a fit.

## TABLE XIII

### Effect of colour on the sensitivity range of 16 patients tested with the eyes open

| Patient No. | COLOUR | | | |
|:---:|:---:|:---:|:---:|:---:|
| | White | Red | Blue | Green |
| 1 | 43 | 39 | 37 | 44 |
| 2 | 3 | 4 | 0 | 2 |
| 3 | 44 | 40 | 43 | 49 |
| 4 | 4 | 0 | 1 | 1 |
| 5 | 1 | 3 | 1 | 1 |
| 6 | 30 | 23 | 28 | 30 |
| 7 | 39 | 36 | 36 | 40 |
| 8 | 47 | 40 | 40 | 42 |
| 9 | 2 | 1 | 0 | 1 |
| 10 | 56 | 42 | 53 | 52 |
| 11 | 31 | 41 | 4 | 34 |
| 12 | 1 | 22 | 1 | 3 |
| 13 | 38 | 35 | 1 | 35 |
| 14 | 1 | 5 | 0 | 0 |
| 15 | 48 | 36 | 48 | 48 |
| 16 | 2 | 1 | 3 | 1 |

## Colour

Since many authors have suggested that the colour of the flashing light is an important factor in precipitating photoconvulsive responses (see page 15) we investigated this factor on a sample of our patients. We were at the time considering improvements in the design of anti-flicker glasses (see page 99), and if we could show a differential response to different hues it would be worth incorporating the appropriate colour filter in the design.

In order to differentiate the effect of colour from changes in intensity produced by interposing a coloured filter between the lamp and the patient, a special hood was constructed which fitted over the Grass photostimulator. The hood contained three Fresnel screens and a diffuser, which together ensured that the illumination was even, but the screen facing the patient was 11 inches square, presenting a much larger area of stimulation than used in our previous research. There was a slot in the hood between the photostimulator and the Fresnel screens into which coloured or neutral density filters could be inserted.

Kodak Wratten gelatine filters were used for colour. The colours and the neutral density filters were matched for transmission and were also equated to the photopic response curve of the human eye. The colours used were red 25, light blue 44, green 58. All the filters were mounted in clear plastic slides.

In this investigation there were 10 patients from Group I, 4 from Group III, and 2 patients who showed photoconvulsive responses to IPS but had no history of epilepsy. One of these latter patients was the sister of a clinically photosensitive patient, and the other was a female with syncopal attacks. There were 6 males and 10 females, with a mean age of 14.2 years. All the patients were investigated in both the eyes open and eyes closed condition for each colour, and their sensitivity ranges established by standard methods.

The width of the sensitivity range to white light (photostimulator with a neutral

83

density filter) was taken as the standard for each patient. Many of the patients showed only slight differences in sensitive ranges between the different colours with their eyes open. There was a significant (p. < .01) reduction in sensitivity to blue light (fig. 44), although the sensitivity ranges to the different colours varied among the patients. Only one patient showed a slight increase in sensitivity to blue light (Table XIII). The reduction in sensitivity to blue light was not related to the clinical groups, nor was it related to type of attack.

Overall the patient group showed a slightly reduced sensitivity with red stimulation, but 5 patients showed some increase in sensitivity range. Of these patients one showed a marked increase in sensitivity range from a width of 1 (white) to 22 (red).

Another five patients showed increased sensitivity to green stimulation, and in general this colour was nearest to white light in its effect.

Many patients showed no sensitivity to intermittent photic stimulation with the eyes closed. The two patients who had abnormalities in the eyes-closed condition both showed increased sensitivity to red light and no sensitivity to blue and green. This is probably explained by the red filter of the eyelids.

The colour of the light did not significantly alter the VEP or the presence of occipital spikes.

These findings contrast with most previous published results (Chapter 2). Although other authors have suggested the use of blue-tinted glasses, this has been on the basis of increased sensitivity to red light. A decrease in sensitivity to blue light has not previously been reported in the literature. In part the reason for this difference may be differences in the parameters investigated. We have investigated the effect of colour on sensitivity range, which may be only partially correlated with other authors' parameters such as frequency of occurrence or the latency of photoconvulsive responses.

Our finding that there is no significant difference in the effectiveness of other colours also contrasts with most of the previous literature. Only Rao and Pritchard (1955) suggest that there is no significant difference between white and coloured light. Most authors have suggested increased sensitivity to red light (Walter and Walter 1949, Carterett and Symmes 1952, Livingston 1952, Marshal et al. 1953, Brausch and Ferguson 1962, Pantelakis et al. 1962, Capron 1966).

This discrepancy may be partly due to failure of some authors to control the relative intensities of the filtered lights. Obviously the higher the transmission factor of the filter the greater the intensity of light reaching the retina. Most authors used Kodak Wratten filters, as we have, but where details of the filters are given, the specifications show differences in transmission values.

Our findings of increased sensitivity to red light in the eyes-closed condition may be a further reason for the discrepancy. As discussed in Chapter 2, many authors do not differentiate between the eyes-open, eyes-closed and eye-closure states. If their patients were tested in the eyes-closed and eye-closure conditions an increased sensitivity to red light might well be found, since the eyelid is acting as a red filter which transmits red light, but filters part of the white light and nearly all the blue and green light.

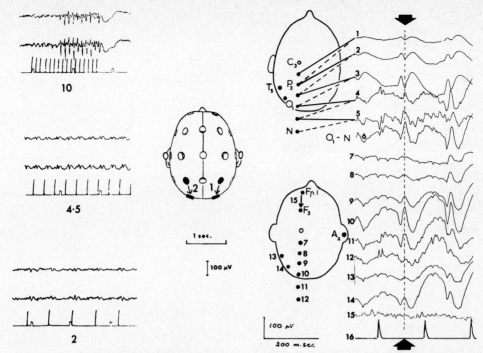

**Fig. 45.** Responses to 3 different flash rates in one patient. At 2 f.sec. there are exaggerated VEP responses, which are also apparent at 4.5 f.sec., giving a pseudo-spike and wave appearance. Occipital spikes are evoked at 10 f.sec.

**Fig. 46.** Localisation of occipital spikes using bipolar and common reference montages and fast paper speed (15 cm/sec.). Vertical dotted line crosses the negative occipital spike. In the bipolar montage (channels 1-6) the negative occipital spike shows phase reversal to the occipital electrode ($O_1$). In the common reference recording (channels 7-14) the highest amplitude of the negative occipital spike is seen in the occipital derivation (channel 10). Flash rate channel 16. (From Panayiotopoulos *et al.* 1972.)

We also studied the effect of colour on the VEPs of a small normal sample population. Surprisingly, two of the 25 subjects showed photoconvulsive responses to IPS. Neither of these subjects had any clinical or familial history of epilepsy or even 'fainting' attacks. Both were female and one showed a sensitivity range of 4 flash frequencies and one of 44. Whether this high percentage of abnormality in the population is related to the efficiency of the larger and more powerful photostimulator is uncertain.

**Occipital spikes and the VEP**

Although abnormalities confined to the occipital regions have occasionally been reported by some authors, they are rare in comparison with the large number of reports of generalised photoconvulsive responses.

The first report of a high incidence of occipital spikes in photosensitive patients

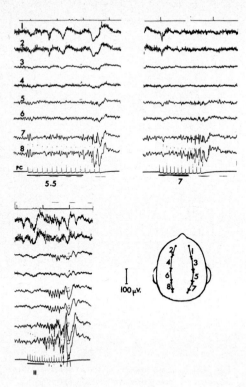

**Fig. 47.** As the flash rate is increased the occipital spikes occur earlier in the train of flashes. (From Panayiotopoulos 1972.)

was that of Hishikawa *et al.* (1967) who found occipital spikes in over 50 per cent of their patient group.

We had observed peculiar responses in the occipital derivations of some of our patients when they were stimulated by IPS at low flash rates (Jeavons 1969). These appeared to be either a supra-normal visual evoked potential or some distortion of the VEP giving the appearance of pseudo-spike and wave (fig. 45). In order to clarify their significance an initial investigation was carried out using a slight modification of our standard EEG procedure.

*Initial study of occipital spikes*

The EEG studies were all carried out using an Elema Schönander 16-channel machine. This machine had the advantage of high paper speeds of 15, 30 and 60 cm./sec. By combining this high paper speed with increased gains (50, 30 and 20 $\mu$V/cm.) we were able to display the occipital spikes in greater detail, and special montages allowed us to study their location and spread. These montages consisted of a special VEP montage (Harding *et al.* 1969) and a montage giving simultaneous common reference and bipolar recording of the occipital spike. Thirty-eight consecutive patients with a clinical history of photosensitive epilepsy (Groups I and II) and 16 patients of Group III were used for this study.

*Results:* From our EEG observations it was apparent that the occipital spike induced by IPS had a main component which was negative at the occipital electrode.

Preceding this negative component was a small positive deflection and following it was a further positive component. The most obvious and constant component was the occipitally negative deflection (fig. 11).

The polarity and localisation of the occipital spikes were confirmed using additional scalp electrodes and sub-occipital electrodes (fig. 46). As can be seen from this figure, in common reference recording the maximal amplitude is obtained from the occipital derivation and on bipolar recording the occipital spikes show phase reversal to the occipital electrode.

The occipital spikes first appear in the EEG between 200 m.sec. and 3 seconds after the onset of a train of intermittent photic stimulation, but never appear in response to the first flash. As the flash rate was increased the first occipital spike tended to occur earlier (fig. 47). In most patients the occipital spikes progressively increased in amplitude in response to subsequent flashes (see fig. 11), reaching a maximum after 3-9 flashes, and then either declining in amplitude (fig. 48) or terminating in a PCR (fig. 49). This waxing and waning of the occipital spike was more likely to occur at lower flash rates (5-7 f.sec.) while termination in a generalised discharge usually occurred at higher flash rates. The rate of occurrence of the occipital spikes was fundamentally related to the flash rate, although in a few patients the spikes induced by relatively low rates of flash (less than 7 f.sec.) were intermittent. In one patient high rates of flash produced occipital spikes at the first subharmonic (fig. 50).

The amplitude of the negative occipital spike was usually between 60 and 100 $\mu$V but occasionally exceeded 150 $\mu$V. The occipital spikes were usually symmetrical although in a few cases they were of higher amplitude in one hemisphere. They usually disappeared or diminished when IPS was given with the patient's eyes closed. Monocular stimulation was less effective in producing occipital spikes.

Of the 38 patients with photosensitive epilepsy, 33 showed occipital spikes in the EEG, preceding a generalised photoconvulsive discharge. In 22 of these patients the occipital spikes appeared at low flash rates (4-10 f.sec.) either alone or preceding the PCR. Since the period of IPS was restricted to two seconds, it is probable that lower frequencies would have evoked both occipital spikes and PCRs if longer trains of stimuli had been given. In the other 11 patients the photoconvulsive responses were elicited by flash rates higher than 11 f.sec. and were immediately preceded by occipital spikes. The remaining 5 of the 38 patients did not show any occipital spikes preceding the PCR. However, two of these patients showed PCRs to flash rates as low as 1 f.sec.

Of the 16 patients from Group III, 15 showed occipital spikes in response to IPS. Twelve of the 15 showed spikes preceding a PCR and 3 showed occipital spikes alone. The sixteenth patient showed PCRs without preceding occipital spikes.

*Occipital spikes and VEP*

Since Hishikawa *et al.* (1967) had suggested that the occipital spikes were augmented components of the visual evoked potentials we decided to study the relationship between the occipital spikes and the VEP of the patients, and compare these findings with those obtained from a normal control group. The patients were 20

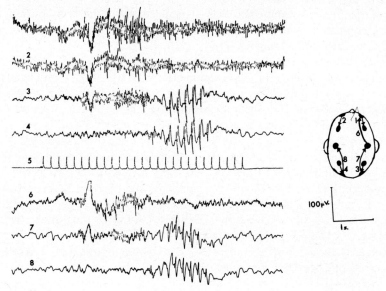

**Fig. 48.** Occipital spikes increasing and decreasing in amplitude and disappearing during a continuous period of stimulation. (From Panayiotopoulos 1972.)

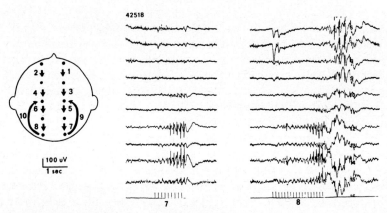

**Fig. 49.** Asymmetrical occipital spikes occur in isolation in response to 7 f.sec., but at 8 f.sec. the occipital spikes terminate in a PCR.

of those used in the EEG study and there were 18 normal controls with the same mean age. In order to obtain clear visual evoked potential, and accurate measurement of the latency of the occipital spikes, an averager (CAT 400 C) was used.

The technique of averaging operates on the assumption that the evoked potential will be time-locked to the stimulus, whereas the background noise of the EEG will be random in its relationship. Thus, if a stimulus is repetitively presented and the EEG on each occasion is stored, the common features will slowly add together to produce a clearer 'evoked potential', while the random noise which contains all possible phases of both positive and negative waves will slowly approximate to zero (see fig. 4). An

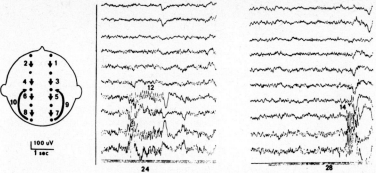

**Fig. 50.** Occipital spikes at 12 per second in response to flicker at 24 f.sec., and a similar subharmonic response to 28 f.sec.

inherent disadvantage of this technique is that it provides the average of a number of discrete responses to a stimulus and does not differentiate between the first response and, say, the twentieth. An added disadvantage is that it assumes that the background EEG is entirely random and unrelated to the stimulus, which is not true (Goldstein 1970). Other studies have demonstrated that the evoked potential is intimately related to the spontaneous EEG (Spilker *et al.* 1969).

The four channels of the CAT were used, the first two recording the right and left occipito-central derivations ($O_2$ - $C_4$, $O_1$ - $C_3$ respectively). Although these are bipolar derivations, the right and left central electrodes may be regarded as relatively inactive in relation to a visual evoked potential. The third channel ($C_4$ - $Fp_2$) was used to monitor eye movements in case EOG artifact affected either the VEP or occipital spike write-out. The fourth channel was used to display the output of a photocell (placed alongside the subject's head) to each flash of the photostimulator. The output of the photocell was also used to trigger each sweep of the CAT. Although the photocell responded to each flash of the photostimulator the CAT, of course, could only be triggered by the next flash following the conclusion of its sampling sweep.

Between 22 and 200 sweeps were averaged to obtain the VEP, the sweep time being either 250 or 500 m.sec. The same length of sweep was used for the occipital spikes, but fewer sweeps were averaged (25 or less). The latency of both the occipital spikes and the visual evoked potentials was measured from the beginning of the preceding flash to the point of maximum amplitude.

*Results:* The initial positive wave of the occipital spike had a latency of 87.5 m.sec. ($\pm 11.5$ m.sec.). Its latency appeared constant irrespective of flash rate between 4.5 and 10 f.sec. The latency remained unchanged even when the interval between flashes was shorter than the latency of the negative spike (fig. 51). It can be seen from this figure that as the interval between flashes becomes smaller (i.e. the flash rate increases) it equals and then becomes less than the latency of the occipital spike at low flash rates. Either the occipital spike must have shown a marked reduction in latency, or it was the response to the preceding flash but one. The latter explanation is more likely. The occipital spikes and VEPs of the 20 patients were examined using this method, and the latency of the occipital spikes compared to the latency of the $N_2$ and

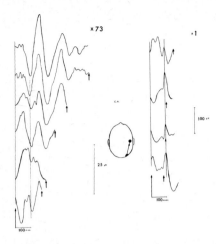

**Fig. 51.** Comparison between the VEP and occipital spike of a photosensitive patient. The latency of the negative occipital spike (right) is consistent (100 m.sec.) irrespective of the flash frequency, even when the flash interval is less than the latency of the occipital spike (flash rates, from the top downwards, 6.5, 9, 10, 11 f.sec.). The vertical line which crosses the VEP (left) is at the mean latency of the occipital spikes and does not coincide with any negative VEP components evoked by 1-6 f.sec. (shown by vertical arrows). The VEP is the average of 73 sweeps. (From Panayiotopoulos *et al.* 1972.)

$P_2$ components of their respective VEPs obtained in response to IPS at 1-4 f.sec. The mean latency for the $N_2$ component was 79 m.sec. and for the $P_2$ component 110 m.sec.

In 18 of the 20 patients the latency of the negative occipital spike did not coincide with the latency of any negative components of the VEP. In the remaining 2 patients the $P_2$ component was triphasic and the negative occipital spike appeared to be related to the latency of the negative triphasic component of $P_2$ (component 5b of Gastaut and Regis 1964). In one of these two patients the negative triphasic wave of the $P_2$ component ($P_2$b) increased in amplitude as the flash rate increased, finally becoming the negative occipital spike (fig. 52). It was of interest that in 9 of the 18 patients the latency of the occipital spikes coincided with the latency of the $P_2$ component of the VEP.

In the normal subjects the visual evoked potentials to IPS from 1-4 f.sec. show an $N_2$ component with a mean latency of 81 m.sec. and a $P_2$ component with a latency of 110 m.sec. When the flash rate was increased to 5-10 f.sec., the latency of the $N_2$ component was increased to 86 m.sec. and the latency of the $P_2$ component to 114 m.sec. (fig. 53). In all normal subjects the latencies of $N_2$ and $P_2$ were constant at flash rates between 1 and 4 f.sec., and in 9 subjects the latency of these components was constant at all flash rates. Four of the remaining 9 showed constant latency of the $P_2$ component but variable latency of $N_2$ at higher flash rates (5-10 f.sec.). In a further 4 subjects both the $N_2$ and $P_2$ latency were different at high flash rates when compared to low, and in the remaining subject the $N_2$ component was constant, but the latency of $P_2$ increased with higher flash rates.

In summary, no negative VEP components seen in normal controls or patients showed similar latencies to the negative occipital spike. Thus the suggestion of Hishikawa *et al.* (1967) that the occipital spike is an augmentation of early negative components of the VEP cannot be supported. However, in two patients the occipital spike showed a clear relation to the $P_2$b component and in a further 9 patients the latency of the negative occipital spike coincided with the latency of the $P_2$ component

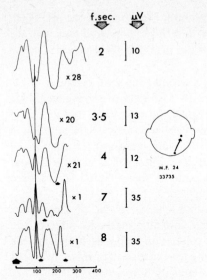

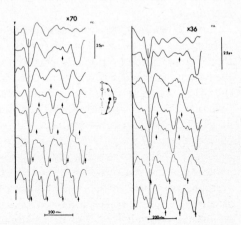

**Fig. 52.** Development of occipital spike from component $P_2b$ of VEP in a patient. As the flash rate is increased from 2 to 8 f.sec., component $P_2b$ increases in amplitude to become the negative occipital spike. (From Panayiotopoulos *et al.* 1970.)

**Fig. 53.** VEPs in response to 1-10 f.sec. obtained from two normal subjects. The arrows indicate flash instant and the vertical lines cross the $P_2$ components. Number of averaging sweep indicated at top. (From Panayiotopoulos *et al.* 1972.)

of the VEP. In one of the patients the negative occipital spike appeared to develop from the negative $P_2b$ component of the VEP as the flash rate was increased.

*Occipital spikes and the $P_2b$ component*

Since it appeared possible that the $P_2b$ component was either intimately related to the occipital spike, or was even the undeveloped form of the spike, it was decided to investigate the relationship. This study was carried out on 46 patients; 21 were from Group I, 15 from Group II, 8 from Group III and there were two patients who had no history of epileptic attacks. One of the latter was the identical twin of a photosensitive patient and the other had a history of migraine. Both of these patients produced photoconvulsive responses to IPS.

The techniques used in this study were a combination of those used in the first VEP study and those used in the study of the effect of pattern. All patients were examined using a Grass photostimulator fitted with a diffuser and a removable fine grid pattern, each square subtending 22' of visual angle. This was the grid which had been found most effective in producing photoconvulsive responses in the pattern study (see page 77). The intensity of the photostimulator was kept at 68 nit/second. In order to increase the accuracy of the measurement of latencies of the occipital spike and small components of the VEP, the sampling rate of the CAT was twice that used in the previous study. To obtain this increased sample rate using a computer with a fixed number of stores, the number of channels averaged was reduced. One channel of the averager was used for either the right or left occipito-central derivation

91

$O_2$ - $C_4$ or $O_1$ - $C_3$, and one channel was used to monitor the output of the photocell. The patients received IPS in the binocular state with diffuser alone and then with the addition of the grid, but in the monocular state the grid and diffuser were always combined.

*Results:* When both eyes were stimulated with IPS without the grid, occipital spikes were seen in the basic EEG of only 7 of the 46 patients. Using the averaging technique these 7 and a further 5 patients showed occipital spikes in their VEP, and in half of them occipital spikes could be observed at flash rates as low as 1 f.sec. The addition of the grid pattern to the Grass photostimulator markedly increased the number of patients showing occipital spikes. Thirty-one showed occipital spikes in the EEG and 42 showed occipital spikes in the VEP. In 26 patients the occipital spikes were observable at 1 f.sec.

Four of the 46 patients did not show occipital spikes. In one of these four, photoconvulsive responses were evoked by 1 f.sec. and this markedly affected the averaged response. In the 3 other patients no explanation could be found for the absence of occipital spikes, although it is interesting to note that all of them produced an absence with bilateral 3 c.sec. spike and wave activity in response to IPS.

When the averaged responses to IPS at low flash rates were examined in detail it became apparent that there was a constant relation between the $P_2b$ component of the VEP and the occipital spike. In general the negative occipital spike appeared on the descending portion of the $P_2$ component of the VEP (fig. 54). The mean latency of the negative occipital spike for the patients was 91 m.sec. (standard deviation 3.5 m.sec.). The mean latency for the $N_2$ component of the VEP was 58 m.sec. (standard deviation 3.4 m. sec.) and for the $P_2$ component 111 m.sec. (standard deviation 3.6 m.sec.). Both the occipital spike and the $P_2$ component of the VEP showed consistent latencies in each individual, irrespective of the flash rate. The use of the grid pattern did of course allow the precipitation of occipital spikes at lower rates of IPS ($< 8$ f.sec.) than in the initial study.

The presence or absence of the occipital spike and its amplitude were clearly related to the presence or absence of the grid and the rate of IPS (fig. 55). When the grid was present, the occipital spike appeared at low flash rates and showed increasing amplitude with increase of flash rate. In some patients with a low limit to their sensitivity range, the occipital spike appeared to replace the $P_2b$ component and dominate the VEP as the flash rate was increased. When the diffuser was used alone and the flash rate was low, the occipital spike did not appear or was of low amplitude or inconsistent.

On monocular stimulation using the grid pattern the occipital spike was markedly reduced in amplitude in the VEP, and was often no longer apparent in the EEG even when relatively high rates of IPS were given (fig. 56).

*Discussion*

It is apparent from the results of the above studies that the occipital spike is more commonly seen than was previously reported, and is a consistent phenomenon in the VEPs of nearly all photosensitive patients. The discrepancy between our findings and those of other authors may be attributable to certain aspects of our technique. The

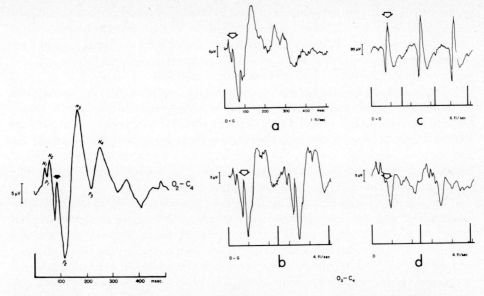

**Fig. 54.** VEP of patient with negative occipital spikes (arrowed) on the decending phase of the $P_2$ component. (From Harding and Dimitrakoudi.)

**Fig. 55.** Effect of increasing flash rate, with grid pattern, on the amplitude of the occipital spike. (a) At 1 f.sec. a small occipital spike (arrowed) can be seen during the descending phase of the $P_2$ component, when the grid is present; (b) With increase of flash rate to 4 f.sec., there is an increase in the amplitude of the occipital spike; (c) At 6 f.sec. the occipital spike dominates the VEP (note that the gain has had to be reduced from 5 to 20 $\mu$v.); (d) With diffuser only (grid having been removed) the occipital spike, or $P_2$b component, can scarcely be seen. (From Harding and Dimitrakoudi.)

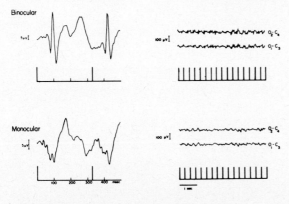

**Fig. 56.** Effect of binocular and monocular stimulation on occipital spikes. With binocular stimulation high amplitude occipital spikes are present in the VEP and EEG. With monocular stimulation only a small $P_2$ occurs in the VEP and no occipital spikes can be seen in the EEG. (From Harding and Dimitrakoudi.)

combination of a diffusion screen, a fine grid pattern and high intensity light appears to result in a highly provocative stimulus for photosensitive patients. It is clearly apparent that the occipital spike is intimately related to the $P_2$b component and that the presence of this component is more common in the VEPs of photosensitive patients, as suggested by Gastaut and Regis (1964).

It would therefore appear possible that the mechanisms which are involved in the production of the earlier components of the VEP may also subserve the production of the occipital spike. If positive components ($P_2$) of the VEP are produced by inhibitory post-synaptic potentials (Creutzfeldt and Kuhnt 1967), then the latency similarities between the negative occipital spike and the $P_2$ component could be interpreted as a failure of normal inhibitory mechanisms in these patients.

The findings on the effect of patterns support the suggestion that the mechanisms producing the earlier component of the VEP and the occipital spike are the same. Patterned stimuli, which are said to involve more cortical neurones (Hubel and Wiesel 1968) and which enhance the amplitude of the evoked potential, also increase the amplitude of the occipital spike. Furthermore, factors which reduce the number of cortical neurones involved, such as diffusion of light, monocular stimulation, or blue light, also reduce the amplitude of the negative occipital spike.

These findings suggest that while the pathways involved in the production of the primary VEP and the occipital spike are the same, the occurrence of the occipital spike is a manifestation of the failure of the visual cortex to react to a massive stimulus in a normal physiological manner. Since occipital spikes are frequently seen in these patients as a precursor to photoconvulsive responses, it appears likely that intermittent photic stimulation is producing a focal occipital abnormality which may then trigger a secondary generalised discharge.

CHAPTER 8

# Therapy

## Anticonvulsants

A number of patients are already receiving anticonvulsants when they are first referred for EEG and in such cases one cannot draw any conclusions about the effect of the drug on abnormalities evoked by photic stimulation. We have examined 44 patients in whom an EEG was obtained both before and after the introduction of a drug. A number of these patients were not under our clinical care. Twenty-three recently received sodium valproate ('Epilim') as part of a preliminary trial into the value of this drug in the management of the photosensitive patient. Twelve of these 23 patients had already failed to respond to other anticonvulsants but 11 had never received any drugs before.

Table XIV summarises the effect of anticonvulsants on the abnormalities evoked by IPS. Although the patients' attacks and their basic EEGs may show improvement in response to anticonvulsant therapy, there may be no change in the response to the potent stimulus of the photostimulator. Since some patients were receiving more than one drug, or had failed to respond to several drugs before taking sodium valproate, the total figures exceed 44, some patients appearing two or three times.

From the table it can be seen that phenobarbitone and phenytoin had little effect. Ethosuximide was effective in less than half the patients who received it; 9 out of 16 continued to show PCRs. Of the 7 patients given ethosuximide in whom EEG abnormalities diminished or disappeared, 5 had responded to IPS by producing an absence. One such patient did not respond to ethosuximide but later responded to sodium valproate.

Sodium valproate has so far proved effective in inhibiting abnormalities evoked by IPS, though it is often necessary to give a relatively large dose to inhibit the PCR completely. Our trial of this drug is continuing and we are giving it to those patients who have a normal basic record and only show spike and wave during IPS. It seems justified to give sodium valproate to such patients because it has not produced unwanted effects, and reducing the photosensitivity makes it possible for the patient

**TABLE XIV**
**The effect of anticonvulsants on abnormalities evoked by IPS**

| Anticonvulsant | No. of patients | EEG improved | EEG no change |
|---|---|---|---|
| Phenobarbitone | 17 | 5 | 12 |
| Phenytoin | 17 | 3 | 14 |
| Ethosuximide | 16 | 7 | 9 |
| Sulthiame | 3 | — | 3 |
| Nitrazepam | 1 | — | 1 |
| Diazepam | 1 | 1 | |
| Troxidome | 1 | 1 | |
| Sodium valproate | 23 | 21 | 2 |

N = 44. Some patients appear more than once.

to lead a life free from restrictions. Since we have some evidence that photosensitivity disappears in later life (see Chapter 9) it will be necessary to stop sodium valproate for a month each year and then repeat the EEG to see if spike and wave discharges can still be evoked by IPS.

**Therapy without drugs**

It is generally agreed that a patient who has a single epileptic fit should not be given anticonvulsants until investigations have been made. If no cause is discovered, and if the EEG is normal or shows only mild non-focal abnormality, anticonvulsants should not be given unless further seizures occur. To attach a label of epilepsy one must have a history of recurrent fits—a single fit is not epilepsy. The patient who has a fit evoked by television or other flickering light does not require drug therapy if the basic EEG is normal and spike and wave discharges are confined to photic stimulation. (The exception may be the use of sodium valproate, see above.)

The therapy for the photosensitive patient, without the use of drugs, is for the patient to avoid the stimulus. All patients in our care who show clear and definite abnormality on IPS and in whom there is a history of precipitation of a fit by flickering light in everyday life are given the following printed instruction sheet.

*Precautions to be taken by patients who are sensitive to flickering lights*

If these instructions are followed carefully and exactly, a fit may be avoided while watching television.

1. The patient should *always* view the television in a well lit room from a distance of 8 feet or more.
2. A small illuminated table lamp should be placed on top of the television set.
3. The patient should *never* be allowed to approach the television to adjust or switch channels of the set.
4. If for some reason the patient has to go near the television, then he/she should cover one eye with the palm of the hand so as not to allow any light to enter the eye.
5. The patient should never attend discotheques or any other places where flashing lights are used, but if any flashing lights come on without warning, he/she should immediately cover one eye with the palm of the hand.
6. The wearing of polarised sunglasses out of doors on sunny days is of assistance in removing flickering reflections (from water, etc.). Ordinary tinted spectacles are of no value in this condition.

The patient is shown how to cover the eye and all patients are also shown the effect of monocular occlusion on their own EEG responses.

Polarised spectacles remove the reflected flicker produced by sunlight on water, snow, or wet surfaces. The patient or parent should be advised to purchase a pair, and in the case of children they should choose their own fashionable ones, as this will help to ensure that they wear them. In the U.K. polarised spectacles can now be prescribed by the consultant in charge of the case, provided that the patient has no significant refractive error.

If the basic EEG shows spontaneous spike and wave discharges it may be necessary to give anticonvulsants, but we do not always do so if fits have only occurred in the presence of flickering light.

Before devising the very simple method of covering the eye with the hand we did advise four patients to use an eye patch. Three of these patients were impulsively attracted to the T.V. set. The most successful result concerned a woman of 26 who was unable to have the T.V. set on in the house, because as soon as she entered the room she would be drawn to the set, jerk and finally convulse (see page 34). She was able to carry on her normal housework with the T.V. set on, provided she wore her light-proof patch. One boy was so offended at the idea of wearing a patch that he managed to overcome the impulsive attraction. The therapy was successful in another child, but failed in the fourth because he would peep round the patch. It is probable that if the impulsive child will not cover his eye with his hand he will not tolerate an eye patch.

## Conditioning

We have attempted conditioning methods of therapy in only 3 patients. In one of our early studies we attempted a safe-limits method of conditioning. The patient, Elaine, aged 6, had frequent tonic-clonic and myoclonic attacks. Our method was based on Hull's (1943) theory of stimulus generalisation and discrimination points. IPS was given to the patient at a flash rate higher than the upper limit of the sensitivity range by an amount equal to the difference between the centre of the sensitivity range and the upper limit. According to Hullian theory, if this flash rate is presented frequently enough without producing a photoconvulsive response, the upper limit of the sensitivity range (which is mid-way between the safe stimulus frequency and the centre of the sensitivity range) should progressively become lower as the ratio of safe stimulus presentation to unsafe stimulus presentation increases. Thus the range will reduce as the upper limit (or discrimination point) is lowered. The safe stimulus flash rate can then be lowered and more conditioning given. In spite of five weeks of conditioning at two sessions of 1½ hours/week the child's sensitivity range at the end of the series was identical to that obtained before conditioning commenced.

The second study was carried out using the method of differential light intensity (Forster and Campos 1964) (see page 28). A photostimulator flanked by two photoflood bulbs whose intensity could be controlled was placed behind a large diffusion screen. A flash rate was established which consistently provoked a photoconvulsive response, and then the photofloods were switched on and their intensity progressively increased until no PCR was produced by photic stimulation. Repeated extinction trials were then given and if no PCR was evoked the intensity of the photofloods was reduced and extinction recommenced. The patient used for our study was a young woman aged 20 with a history of tonic-clonic attacks induced by television viewing (Group I). Having established a provocative flash rate, we increased the level of contrasting illumination of the photofloods and extinction trials began. At this point a PCR was evoked by one second of stimulation, paroxysmal theta activity developed and the patient had a tonic-clonic convulsion. The technique was therefore not repeated.

The third method of conditioning we used was monocular stimulation. The patient, a 14-year-old boy of Group I, showed total inhibition of abnormality when IPS was given monocularly to either eye. During our initial testing it appeared that after a period of monocular stimulation there was a reduction in the amount of abnormality provoked by binocular stimulation. Extinction therapy trials were therefore carried out at a later date using monocular stimulation, but at the conclusion of extinction there was no significant change in the sensitivity to binocular stimulation.

*Discussion*

Our failure with all conditioning methods contrasts with the reports of Forster and his co-workers, but supports the results of Braham (1967). On theoretical grounds it appears to us impossible that these methods should work. While there is no doubt that a conditional stimulus, such as a bell, may become associated with an unconditional stimulus (IPS) in producing a response (PCR), and may become associated to such a degree that in isolation it produces the response, the IPS as unconditional stimulus cannot be extinguished. The association of any conditional stimulus (e.g. bell) may, of course, be extinguished, but conditioning theory does not allow the extinguishing of the unconditional stimulus. Thus for conditioning therapy to work in photosensitive epilepsy the flickering light would have to be the conditional stimulus, which has become associated with an unknown unconditional stimulus.

**Spectacles**

Since environmental modification had proved successful in enabling patients to watch television safely, we attempted to provide some equivalent means of dealing with flickering stimuli in the outside environment. Patients had reported having attacks in relation to flickering sunlight reflected from the sea, snow, and wet streets, and also reported attacks precipitated by sunlight flickering between trees, fences and railings.

The effective factor in 'television' therapy appeared to be reduction of relative intensity by sitting further from the television set in a well lit room, and placing an illuminated lamp on top of or near the television set so that this shone into the patient's eyes. Obviously any therapeutic device, to be successful out of doors, must incorporate similar factors and in addition remove reflected flicker.

The latter factor was the easiest to solve and we advised our patients to wear polarising sunglasses when out of doors on bright days. These proved more effective than simple tinted glasses, presumably because with tinted glasses the eye quickly adapted to the lower levels of intensity by pupil dilation.

The polarised glasses had, of course, no effect on direct flicker. It is very difficult to reduce the apparent intensity of sunlight and it is equally difficult out of doors to reduce the contrast between flickering sunlight and a dark background. We therefore devised a spectacle system which would automatically reduce the intensity of the

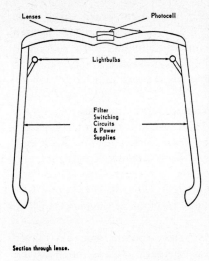

Lenses

Photocell

Lightbulbs

Filter
Switching
Circuits
& Power
Supplies

Section through lense.

Photosensitive absorptive filter
Polarising filter
Optical correction

Eliptical reflecting lense

**Fig. 58.** Photograph of inside of Mark 2 spectacles showing the light bulbs (L.B.) set in the perspex prisms (P).

**Fig. 57** (left). Diagram of Mark 1 spectacles. The filter, matching circuits and power supplies are contained in 'deaf aid' side frames. The light from the bulbs is reflected from the elliptical reflecting lens into the eye. The photosensitive absorptive filter darkens with increases in environmental illumination and the polarising filter removes specular reflections. (From Harding *et al.* 1969).

sunlight as it became brighter, would remove reflected flicker, and would recognise flicker in the environment and provide a bright steady light source to reduce contrast.

*Design of the spectacles*

Flicker in the environment was picked up by a photocell placed on the bridge of the spectacles, which passed the resultant electrical signal to a filter circuit. The filter circuit restricted the response of the system to flicker at flash rates to which the patient was sensitive. If the flicker was within the sensitivity range the steady light source was illuminated, reducing the apparent contrast between the flickering source and other parts of the visual field (fig. 57). As an added refinement a stabilised image of the steady light source was presented to the retina, covering a visual angle of about 20° dependent upon the pupil size. The stimulus therefore involved an area which subserved most of the information channels of the visual system and was locked on to this area, independent of eye movements. A stabilised image was achieved by use of an elliptical reflecting surface having its foci at the centre of rotation of the eye and the position of the light source near the outer canthus. Reflection occurred at an aluminised surface with a reflecting factor of 12.5 per cent. The highly concave reflector was positioned between the spectacle lens and the eye.

The spectacle lens consisted of three components. The first was a photosensitive absorptive lens which reduced the range of brightness encountered and helped compensate for variations in the relation of the secondary stimulating light source and the luminance of the hazardous flicker. It seemed that an overall attenuation was beneficial on sunny days, whereas minimal, if any, attenuation was necessary for indoor situations such as viewing television. The next layer was a thin polarising film designed to exclude the contribution of specular reflections which arose from horizontal surfaces and were often the source of low frequency pulses of high luminance, as for example, in rippling water reflecting sunlight. The third component of the lens was an optical correction incorporating prismatic and dioptic power to correct the patient's refractive error and any residual aberrations induced by oblique viewing through the reflector.

Although the use of a spectacle frame design which completely blocks the temporal peripheral visual field might constitute a safety hazard, protection from stimulation in this direction was thought at that time to be important. For this reason we used thin photosensitive absorptive panels at the side to attenuate brightness, and an aluminised inner surface to equate its transmission with that of the frontal lens system and to reflect the light source approximately towards the pupil. The aluminised film may also slightly enhance the speed of response of the photosensitive absorptive side panels.

There was a rigid wrap-round portion to the frame, and the side was hinged about 25 mm. from the front to produce a folding spectacle. It was, however, far larger when folded than a conventional spectacle.

In our initial studies of 12 patients, the antiflicker glasses removed the photoconvulsive response to IPS in every case. Since the photochromic layer is slow and could not possibly respond to the flash rate of the photostimulator, this was achieved by the contrast illumination of the light bulbs alone. The procedure was that, with the patient wearing the glasses but with the flicker-sensing circuit switched off, we established the frequency which would consistently provoke a PCR. The flicker-sensing circuit was then switched on and IPS was repeated. The provocative flash rate was tested on a number of occasions and then the flicker-detection circuit was switched off. The IPS was then repeated and a PCR obtained.

Although the glasses were found to be entirely effective they were not cosmetically attractive. In addition, the construction of the spherical half-silvered mirrors was difficult and some simpler method of providing a relatively stabilised illumination in front of the pupil was desirable. We therefore began working on a modified design.

The main problem in simplifying construction was to provide an alternative means of channelling light into the eyes in such a way that its effectiveness would be independent of eye position. A thin plate of clear perspex (1/16″) was fastened to the rear of the spectacle frame, and the edge of the clear perspex was ground to give a 45° prism which passed obliquely in front of the centre of the eye. The spectacle frame was fairly thick and was drilled, and two bulbs were positioned one above and one below the joint of the side frame (fig. 58). Channels were drilled in the frame to connect the bulbs in series using the the side frames as part of the circuit. The bulbs were 3 mm. tubular wire-ended vitality bulbs. They require a supply of 5 volts 0.05 amps which gives a life of 100,000 hours. Holes were drilled in the perspex plate so that this fitted over the two bulbs on each side. Thus when the bulbs were illuminated the light was internally reflected in the thin perspex plate, and then reflected off the 45° prism into the eye. The oblique prism was positioned to bisect the pupil, but complete light stabilisation could not be achieved, and a compromise was reached in which the light was stabilised with respect to eye movement in the majority of inferior and superior

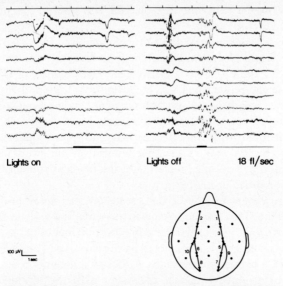

Lights on          Lights off          18 fl/sec

100 μV |
       | 1 sec

**Fig. 59.** The effect of illuminating the spectacle light bulbs. When the patient is wearing the spectacles with light bulbs switched off a PCR is rapidly evoked by IPS. When the bulbs light up, even a longer period of IPS evokes no abnormality.

positions. Since the prismatic edge was narrow there was minimal interference with normal vision.*

A pilot study was carried out to assess the most appropriate voltage at which to run the spectacle bulbs. It was decided to use amplitude of the $P_2$ component of the VEP of a normal subject as a measure of the effectiveness of the steady illumination in reducing the response to IPS. Frequencies of 1 and 8 flashes per second were used, and the VEP was recorded with the spectacle lights on and off. The voltage of the bulbs was varied between 0 and 20 in 5 volt steps. As the bulbs were connected in series their life was not significantly reduced even when the highest voltage was used. The results showed reduction in the $P_2$ component of the VEP, which was most marked at the full voltage of 20 volts. This voltage was therefore used in assessing the efficiency of the new glasses.

In each investigation a test frequency was used which consistently evoked a PCR in each of the patients investigated (usually between 16 and 20 f/sec.). The intensity of the photostimulator at the chosen test frequency was set to the minimum level which consistently evoked a PCR, since environmental precipitants seen outside the laboratory are of lower intensity than the photostimulator. The Grass photostimulator was used, usually at setting 4, that is 96 nit seconds. On some occasions a neutral density 0.5 filter was used to reduce the illumination. At least four presentations of the photostimulator were given in each of the conditions. In the first condition the spectacle lights were switched off, and in the second condition the spectacle lights

*U.K. Patent Application 17243/69.

101

were illuminated at the same moment as IPS was given. The presentations were arranged in an A B B A design.

Ten patients were investigated, all of whom showed consistent photoconvulsive responses to IPS. Eight of the patients came from Group I, and two from Group III. Seven were female, and all had previously been investigated.

In every case the re-designed spectacles entirely inhibited the photoconvulsive response (fig. 59). The response was inhibited not only at our standard length of stimulation, but even when the length of stimulation was markedly increased. The spectacles had an equally marked effect on occipital spikes when these were present. In each case the occipital spike was either reduced in amplitude or was completely inhibited, and this may be some indication of the mode of action of the spectacles in preventing abnormalities in the EEG.

In the event, a final version of the spectacles was never produced for use by patients out of doors. This was not owing to any complications in design, but to the finding that covering one eye was effective in most patients in preventing attacks. The remaining patients who were not protected by the covering of one eye were found to be controlled by the use of sodium valproate. Although it does not seem worthwhile to go to the expense of producing special spectacles with the illumination device, the photo-chromic layer remains a useful therapy for patients who are markedly sensitive to changes in outside illumination, such as occur on going from a dark room into bright sunlight.

# CHAPTER 9

# Prognosis

Although our first patients were seen in 1961 the decision to carry out annual EEG examination of patients was not made until 1968. As a result we have very few patients in whom the period of follow-up is greater than six years. Therefore we are not yet able to provide reliable data on the prognosis of photosensitive epilepsy. Furthermore, since our studies have often been sequential, changes in technique have made accurate comparison difficult. Throughout these studies our chief concern has been the improvement of the diagnostic procedure and therefore the techniques used have been systematically changed and improved over the years. Whenever possible we have endeavoured to use the original techniques in follow-up investigations.

One can surmise that photosensitivity will disappear with age since it is uncommon to find abnormality in the EEGs of the parents of photosensitive children, even when the parent describes past symptoms associated with flicker. However, only a few of our patients have ceased to show abnormal discharges during IPS during the period of follow-up, although several are in their twenties. In a few patients we have observed spontaneous reduction in sensitivity range, and a similar change has recently been observed in response to treatment with sodium valproate.

We have made a preliminary analysis of the findings obtained at follow-up from 49 patients, who were aged between 10 and 14 years at the time of their first EEG. This age group was selected since 45 per cent of our patients are in this age range at the onset of their attacks. Since the upper limit has shown considerable variability on repeat investigations (see page 67) we have only studied the alteration in the lower limit. The patients at each year of follow-up were divided into two groups, those who had shown an 'improvement' in lower limit (i.e. the limit was at a higher flash rate)

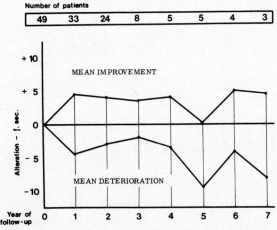

**Fig. 60.** Mean variations in lower limit of photosensitivity over a period of 7 years.

and those who had shown a 'deterioration'. The mean alteration in flash rate was then calculated for each group.

As can be seen from Figure 60, the mean alterations are usually within five flash rates of the initial lower limit. In addition, the alterations in 'improvement' and 'deterioration' are usually approximately equal; thus, on the seven year period, there is no clear evidence of any change. At the seventh year of follow-up the patients would be aged between 17 and 21 years.

All our findings so far suggest that photosensitivity may continue for at least 10 years and that we shall be unable to make a valid assessment of prognosis until we have studied sufficient patients for at least 15 years.

# CHAPTER 10

# Conclusions

Photosensitive epilepsy is not a common condition. However, judging from our findings and those of other authors the incidence of this condition is probably greater than 1 in 10,000. With increasing awareness of 'television epilepsy', the number of children referred for EEG investigation is increasing and probably will continue to do so.

There is little doubt that photosensitivity is more likely to occur, in both sexes, around puberty. Furthermore, there is some evidence that variations in hormonal levels may be a factor in the degree of photosensitivity at any given time. Although little is known of the prognosis of this condition, it is unlikely that spontaneous recovery occurs before the age of twenty. It is however uncommon to find abnormal responses in the EEGs of the parents of photosensitive children, even when their past clinical history suggests that they may have been photosensitive.

## Clinical findings

From the clinical point of view it seems important to differentiate patients whose attacks only occur in response to flickering light from those whose attacks are all apparently 'spontaneous'. Some, of course, have spontaneous attacks and also attacks precipitated by flickering light, and we therefore divided our cases into 3 groups—flicker sensitive, 'spontaneous' and mixed. The 'spontaneous' group included only patients who showed an abnormal response to photostimulation and in whom there was no clinical evidence to suggest that fits had ever been precipitated by flickering light in an everyday situation.

The most common type of fit induced by flickering light is a tonic-clonic seizure.

The commonest precipitant of a fit in our patients was television viewing (66 per cent). Previous authors have suggested that the important factor was abnormal function of the T.V. set, with associated slow flicker. In our experience the factor is *not* the rate of slow flicker, but the nearness of the patient to the set. Any approach to the set, whether to correct a fault or simply change channels or switch off, is enough to precipitate an attack. As has been pointed out by Bower (1963) and Troupin (1966), 'television epilepsy' is less common in the U.S.A. than in Europe, owing to the difference in the frequency of the A.C. mains supply, which is 50 Hz in Europe and 60 Hz in the U.S.A. Since the normally functioning T.V. set produces flicker at the mains frequency and at half that rate, these authors concluded that more patients were sensitive to 25 f.sec. than 30 f.sec. As we have shown, it is the fast flicker rate (50 or 60 f.sec.) that is important, only 22 per cent of patients being sensitive to 60 f.sec.

A surprising finding was that 30 (7 per cent) of the patients were impulsively attracted to the television screen. This symptom presents a particular problem in therapy, in that these patients cannot be treated satisfactorily by any other method than anticonvulsants. It is of interest that males predominate among these patients, which distinguishes this group from all other photosensitive patients and also from those with so-called 'self-induced' epilepsy.

Flickering sunlight precipitated fits in only 7 per cent of our patients, the commonest cause being reflections off water. Although a few patients had experienced unpleasant sensations, jerking, or (very rarely) a fit while travelling as a passenger in a car along an avenue of trees or past railings, with the sun shining from the side, we have no evidence that the driver of a car has ever been affected, despite extensive enquiry from colleagues.

In 1971 we wrote to the *Lancet* asking for any reports of drivers having fits induced by flickering sunlight, and a single case was reported (Barton, personal communication 1971). The patient was driving in the U.S.A. along a straight tree-lined avenue directly into the sun with the trees overhanging the road. His basic EEG was normal and there was no report of the responses to IPS. We think it is possible for sunlight flicker to be a risk if the patient is driving directly into the sun after rain, since in these circumstances there could be reflections and flicker stimulation of the macula. However, if the patient wears polarised spectacles which are also tinted, the risk will be reduced. Another possible hazard is headlights at night but we have no factual evidence that this has caused a driver to have a fit. Here the possible risk could be minimised by keeping the internal light of the car on, thus reducing relative intensity. Thus, if a patient has a normal basic record, has only had a fit induced by the flicker of television, and only shows EEG abnormality when staring directly into the lamp of the photostimulator, we would regard him as safe to have a driving licence. If such patients can be rendered immune to the effects of photic stimulation by the use of sodium valproate there would appear to be no risk at all, provided the testing of the effects of IPS has been carried out using the method we describe.

### EEG studies

Spike and wave discharges were seen in the basic EEGs of 54 per cent of all cases, there being little difference between the three clinical groups. The presence of basic abnormality is important as regards therapy, since those without 'spontaneous' spike and wave discharges do not usually need anticonvulsant therapy (the exception being sodium valproate). Even those with brief (less than 3 secs.) spike and wave discharges in the basic record may not need anticonvulsants if their attacks have only been precipitated by flickering light, or they have had only a single fit.

The finding of spike and wave discharges immediately following eye closure is a reliable indication that abnormality will occur on photic stimulation.

Photic stimulation evokes a variety of responses in the EEG, which have different clinical significance. Photomyoclonic responses, confined to the anterior regions, are rare and of no proven clinical significance. Responses confined to the posterior regions are mainly physiological and include photic driving and visual evoked potentials. Occipital spikes alone are not common and must be regarded as abnormal. Their presence is probably related to the degree of pattern and contrast in the photostimulus. They do not seem to be specific to photosensitive epilepsy and may be seen in non-epileptic conditions (Maheshwari and Jeavons 1975). They frequently precede photoconvulsive responses in patients with photosensitive epilepsy and may help to elucidate the pathophysiology. Since occipital spikes appear to be affected by the same factors (pattern, intensity, direction of gaze, monocular or binocular stimulation) which affect normal physiological responses such as photic driving and the visual evoked potential, it is possible that they represent some failure of natural inhibitory mechanisms in the visual cortex. Thus the occipital spike may act as a temporary epileptogenic focus in precipitating the photoconvulsive response.

Photoconvulsive responses are widespread, bilateral and involve anterior and posterior regions. The commonest response is a spike and wave discharge with a 3 c.sec. slow wave component, but theta spike and wave, polyspikes or spikes at the same rate as the flash may occur. Photoconvulsive responses are a clear indication of photosensitivity. However, a diagnosis of photosensitive epilepsy should only be made if the patient has had a fit induced by flickering light or pattern in his normal environment. Many patients with 'spontaneous' fits show a photoconvulsive response (Group III), and they should not be diagnosed on the EEG findings as suffering from photosensitive epilepsy.

Photoconvulsive responses may be found in the symptom-free siblings of children with photosensitive epilepsy, and very rarely in normal subjects. This latter finding indicates photosensitivity to the massive, provocative stimulus used in the laboratory and it is entirely possible that the individual may never encounter such a powerful stimulus in the outside world.

The establishment of the lowest and highest flash rate that consistently induces a PCR has several advantages. It enables one to define the flash rates at which the individual may be at risk, and to evaluate any improvement or deterioration in his condition (provided the test circumstances are standardised), and it establishes the flicker rates which are of most danger to the photosensitive population.

While a few patients experience an unpleasant sensation associated with a PCR, the commonest clinical abnormality evoked by IPS is myoclonic jerking of eyelids, face or whole body. In spite of the extremely provocative nature of the photostimulator it is extremely rare that a tonic-clonic seizure is provoked using our method. An absence, which commonly lasts between 5 and 15 seconds, may be induced by IPS. Patients in whom an absence is induced show certain characteristics which differentiate them from the rest of those with photosensitive epilepsy.

### Therapy

In our experience the most effective therapy for the photosensitive patient is the avoidance of the stimulus conditions which provoke the fit. Thus, in 'television epilepsy' the patient must not view at close range, nor approach the set to switch or adjust the controls, and the set should always be viewed in well-lit surroundings.

The flicker-sensitive patient should always cover one eye in the presence of flicker if the situation cannot be avoided. All photosensitive patients should wear polarised spectacles in sunny weather. Tinted glasses are of little value unless they are blue.

Patients who are photosensitive only do not usually need anticonvulsant therapy, and most anticonvulsants do not produce a consistent improvement in photo-sensitivity. Preliminary investigation indicates that sodium valproate does diminish

**TABLE XV**

**Factors standardised in photic stimulation**

Briefing of patient
Type of photostimulator
Environmental illumination
Light intensity and colour
Transmission and diffusion
Distance from light source
Direction of gaze
State of eyes
Rates of flash
Duration of stimulus

the degree of photosensitivity, and the absence of side effects may justify its use in such patients.

Patients with photosensitive epilepsy who show spike and wave discharges in their basic EEG, or those with 'spontaneous' fits as well as flicker-induced fits (Group II) may need anticonvulsants, and here the drug of choice appears to be sodium valproate.

## Procedure

Although our method of photic stimulation is extremely safe, it is also most effective in identifying the photosensitive patient. It is essential that the method is standardised (see Table XV) and accurately controlled. A test flash rate (16 f.sec.) should be used to identify the photosensitive patient and in such patients subsequent stimulation should be given in both the 'eyes-open' and 'eyes-closed' condition. Eye closure during photic stimulation is rarely needed and is more likely to provoke a fit. The majority of patients are more sensitive with eyes open than with eyes closed.

The duration of the flicker in the photosensitive patient should be reduced as far as possible and two seconds of stimulation appears to be sufficient.

The photostimulator should be fitted with a grid pattern (*not* a chequer-board pattern as used by Engel 1974) and have a central fixation target. The patient must look at the centre of the lamp since the evocation of photoconvulsive responses depends on the stimulation of the fovea. A coloured stimulating light does not increase the photosensitivity and a blue light reduces the effectiveness of the stimulus.

The effect of monocular stimulation should be tested in every case, to establish whether covering one eye with the palm of the hand will be effective in protecting the patient from flickering light.

# APPENDIX I

# A Discussion of the Photometric Method

For many reasons, some of which are evident in an earlier publication (Brunette and Molotchnikoff 1970), there is difficulty with physical photometry, although it is more meaningful than the output specified in Joules (i.e. energy), which does not readily yield results in terms of luminance.

Our use of a visual photometer to measure the luminance of a flickering light source might at first sight appear unusual owing to the possible role of brightness enhancement, but the mode of operation of the S.E.I. photometer involved attentuation of the luminance by two log units during the measurement. This had the effect of bringing the critical fusion frequency nearer to the frequency at which the measurements were taken, thus minimising the difficulties. A higher frequency could not be used since our observations of oscilloscope traces showed substantial reduction in pulse size of the Kaiser instrument if the flash frequency was increased. Taking all the factors into account we felt that this method afforded the best way of evaluating the stimulus intensity.

The use of the nit (candella per square metre) as the unit for specifying the luminance of photostimulators appeared to have advantages. For studies of a more analytical nature it may be necessary to use a unit of retinal illumination, and such units are based on the nit and the pupil area. For studies of visual evoked potentials and EEG the 'effective trolland' appears to be the appropriate unit, whereas for the scotopic visual evoked response or electroretinogram the simple 'trolland' should be used. A useful discourse on these units has been given by Le Grande (1968). It should be emphasised that the use of the units of retinal illumination is only appropriate when one wishes to study the CNS without the interfering variable of pupil size. In the present study the primary concern was with the sensitivity of the individual and therefore the simple luminance was the appropriate criterion.

The use of the nit second as a measure of the intensity of a photic stimulus follows logically from the above argument. It should be aplied only to pulses of short duration. If the pulse length is greater than a certain critical time the law of reciprocity no longer applies and this measurement becomes less meaningful. In the absence of any more relevant information the general statement of Le Grande (1968) that summation occurs for the pulses of less than 100 m.sec. must be accepted. The nit second is therefore an appropriate unit for describing individual pulses from commercial photostimulators using Xenon flash tubes.

*For the above discussion on the problem of specifying the intensity of photostimulators, and for the measurements carried out, we are indebted to Mr. N. Drasdo of the Department of Ophthalmic Optics, University of Aston.

APPENDIX II

# Raw Data

| | Group A | Group B | Group C | Group D | Group E | Group F | Group I | Group II | Group III | Total |
|---|---|---|---|---|---|---|---|---|---|---|
| Total | 160 | 99 | 21 | 19 | 33 | 122 | 181 | 151 | 122 | 454 |
| Female | 98 | 61 | 11 | 11 | 23 | 81 | 109 | 95 | 81 | 285 |
| Male | 62 | 38 | 10 | 8 | 10 | 41 | 72 | 56 | 41 | 169 |
| Family hist. photosens epilepsy | 14 | 8 | 1 | 1 | 3 | 11 | 15 | 12 | 11 | 38 |
| *Fits* | | | | | | | | | | |
| Tonic-clonic only | 134 | 56 | 18 | 8 | 19 | 68 | 152 | 83 | 68 | 303 |
| Absence only | 9 | 14 | 2 | 3 | 6 | 25 | 11 | 23 | 25 | 59 |
| Myoclonic only | 3 | 6 | — | 3 | 3 | 2 | 3 | 12 | 2 | 17 |
| Other type only | 5 | 1 | — | — | 1 | 4 | 5 | 2 | 4 | 11 |
| Mixed fits | 10 | 22 | 1 | 5 | 4 | 23 | 11 | 31 | 23 | 65 |
| Myoclonic, all cases | 4 | 13 | — | 5 | 5 | 12 | 4 | 23 | 12 | 39 |
| Self-induced | — | — | 1 | 1 | 3 | — | 1 | 4 | — | 5 |
| Impulsive attraction | 16 | 9 | 2 | 3 | — | — | 18 | 12 | — | 30 |
| Pattern-sensitive | 3 | 1 | 2 | 3 | — | — | 5 | 4 | — | 9 |
| *EEG* | | | | | | | | | | |
| Basic EEG normal | 76 | 40 | 13 | 2 | 17 | 53 | 89 | 59 | 53 | 201 |
| Basic EEG abnormal*** | 84 | 59 | 8 | 17 | 16 | 69 | 92 | 92 | 69 | 253 |
| Eye closure sp.wave** | 31 | 22 | 4 | 7 | 4 | 22 | 35 | 33 | 22 | 90 |
| Basic EEG spikes* | | | | | 4 | 2 | 2 | 4 | 2 | 8 |

*IPS*

|  | 140 | 91 | 20 | 19 | 25 | 106 | 160 | 135 | 106 | 401 |
|---|---|---|---|---|---|---|---|---|---|---|
| 3 c.sec. sp. wave | 140 | 91 | 20 | 19 | 25 | 106 | 160 | 135 | 106 | 401 |
| Theta sp. wave | 11 | 5 | — | — | 6 | 11 | 11 | 11 | 11 | 33 |
| Other | 7 | 3 | 2 | 11 | 2 | 3 | 7 | 5 | 3 | 15 |
| Myoclonic jerks | 36 | 20 | — | 1 | 12 | 16 | 38 | 43 | 16 | 97 |
| Absence induced | 2 | 11 | 1 | — | 3 | 14 | 2 | 15 | 14 | 31 |
| No abnormality | 2 | — | — | — | — | 2 | 3 | — | 2 | 5 |
| Tested for occipital spikes | 88 | 56 | 18 | 6 | 15 | 97 | 106 | 77 | 97 | 280 |
| Occipital spikes present | 58 | 37 | 13 | 4 | 11 | 56 | 71 | 52 | 56 | 179 |
| No occipital spikes | 30 | 19 | 5 | 2 | 4 | 41 | 35 | 25 | 41 | 101 |
| Total limits tested | 108 | 60 | 17 | 9 | 15 | 83 | 125 | 84 | 83 | 292 |
| Eyes open only | 63 | 35 | 8 | 5 | 9 | 56 | 71 | 49 | 56 | 176 |
| Eyes open > eyes closed | 36 | 20 | 8 | 3 | 4 | 11 | 44 | 27 | 11 | 82 |
| Eyes closed only | 3 | — | — | — | — | 2 | 3 | — | 2 | 5 |
| Eyes closed > eyes open | 1 | 3 | — | — | 2 | 8 | 1 | 5 | 8 | 14 |
| Eyes open = eyes closed | 2 | 1 | — | — | — | 3 | 2 | 1 | 3 | 6 |
| Eye closure only | 3 | 1 | 1 | 1 | — | 3 | 4 | 2 | 3 | 9 |
| Total tested monocular | 89 | 54 | 14 | 8 | 15 | 64 | 103 | 77 | 64 | 244 |
| Monocular nil abnormal | 58 | 38 | 8 | 7 | 10 | 43 | 66 | 55 | 43 | 164 |
| Monocular less abnormal | 31 | 14 | 6 | 1 | 4 | 19 | 37 | 19 | 19 | 75 |
| Monocular no effect | — | 2 | — | — | 1 | 2 | — | 3 | 2 | 5 |
| Monocular right inhibited better |  |  |  |  |  |  |  |  |  | 15 |
| Monocular left inhibited better |  |  |  |  |  |  |  |  |  | 14 |
| Monocular right = left |  |  |  |  |  |  |  |  |  | 27 |

***includes ** and *.

# REFERENCES

Adrian, E. D., Matthews, B.H. C. (1934) 'The Berger rhythm: potential changes from the occipital lobes in man. *Brain,* **57,** 355.

Ames, F. R. (1971) ' "Self-induction" in photosensitive epilepsy.' *Brain,* **94,** 781.

——(1974) 'Cinefilm and EEG recording during "hand-waving" attacks of an epileptic, photosensitive child.' *Electroencephalography and Clinical Neurophysiology,* **37,** 301.

Andermann, F. (1971) 'Self-induced television epilepsy.' *Epilepsia,* **12,** 269.

Andermann, K., Berman, S., Cooke, P. M., Dickson, J., Gastaut, H., Kennedy, A., Margerison, J., Pond, D. A., Tizard, J. P. M., Walsh, E. G. (1962) 'Self-induced epilepsy. A collection of self-induced epilepsy cases compared with some other photoconvulsive cases.' *Archives of Neurology,* **6,** 49.

Apuleius (1909) *The Apologia and Florida.* Translated by H. E. Butler, Oxford: Clarendon Press.

Atzev, E. (1962) 'The effect of closing of the eyes upon epileptic activity.' *Electroencephalography and Clinical Neurophysiology,* **14,** 561.

Bablouzian, B. L., Neurath, P. W., Sament, S., Watson, C. W. (1969) 'Detection of photogenic epilepsy in man by summation of evoked scalp potentials.' *Electroencephalography and Clinical Neurophysiology,* **26,** 93.

Bailey, P. E., Harding, G. F. A. (1966) 'An automated output for the B.N.I. low frequency wave analyser.' *Proceedings of the Electrophysiological Technologists' Association,* **13,** 41.

Bergamini, L., Bergamasco, B. (1967) *Cortical Evoked Potentials in Man.* Springfield, Ill.: C. C. Thomas, p. 116.

Bickford, R. G. (1966) 'Human "microflexes" revealed by computer-analysis.' *Neurology,* **16,** 302.

—— Klass, D. W. (1962) 'Stimulus factors in the mechanism of television-induced seizures.' *Transactions of the American Neurological Association,* **87,** 176.

—— —— (1969) 'Sensory precipitation and reflex mechanisms.' *In* Jasper, H. H., Ward., A. A., Pope, A. (Eds.) *Basic Mechanisms of the Epilepsies.* Boston: Little, Brown, p. 543.

——Sem-Jacobsen, C. W., White, P. T., Daly, D. (1952) 'Some observations on the mechanism of photic and photo-Metrazol activation.' *Electroencephalography and Clinical Neurophysiology,* **4,** 275.

——Daly, D., Keith, H. M. (1953) 'Convulsive effects of light stimulation in children.' *American Journal of Diseases of Children,* **86,** 170.

Binnie, C. D., Darby, C. E., Hindley, A. T. (1973) 'Electroencephalographic changes in epileptics while viewing television.' *British Medical Journal,* **iv,** 378.

Bower, B. D. (1963) 'Television flicker and fits.' *Clinical Pediatrics,* **2,** 134.

Braham, J. (1967) 'An unsuccessful attempt at the extinction of photogenic epilepsy.' *Electroencephalography and Clinical Neurophysiology,* **23,** 558.

Brandt, H., Brandt, S., Vollmond, K. (1961) 'EEG response to photic stimulation in 120 normal children.' *Epilepsia,* **2,** 313.

Brausch, C. C., Ferguson, J. H. (1965) 'Color as a factor in lightsensitive epilepsy.' *Neurology,* **15,** 154.

Brazier, M. A. B. (1953) 'A review of physiological mechanisms of the visual system in relation to activation techniques in electroencephalography.' *Electroencephalography and Clinical Neurophysiology,* suppl. 4, 93.

Brežný, I. (1965) 'Visual EEG responses in neurological patients.' Sixth International Congress of Electroencephalography and Clinical Neurophysiology, Vienna, 1965. *EEG-EMG Communicationes,* p. 385.

Broughton, R., Meier-Ewert, K.-H., Ebe, M. (1969) 'Evoked visual, somato-sensory and retinal potentials in photosensitive epilepsy.' *Electroencephalography and Clinical Neurophysiology,* **27,** 373.

Brunette, J. R., Molotchnikoff, S. (1970) 'Calibration of flash-tube photostimulators in electroretinography.' *Vision Research,* **10,** 95.

Capron, E. (1966) 'Etude de divers types de sensibilité électroencéphalographique à la stimulation lumineuse intermittente et leur signification.' Thesis. Paris: Foulon.

Carterette, E. C., Symmes, D. (1952) 'Color as an experimental variable in photic stimulation.' *Electroencephalography and Clinical Neurophysiology,* **4,** 289.

Cernáček, J., Cigánek, L. (1962) 'The cortical electroencephalographic response to light stimulation in epilepsy.' *Epilepsia,* **3,** 303.

Chao, D. (1962) 'Photogenic and self-induced epilepsy.' *Journal of Pediatrics.* **61,** 733.

Charlton, M. H., Hoefer, P. F. (1964) 'Television and epilepsy.' *Archives of Neurology,* **11,** 239.

Chatrian, G. E., Lettich, E., Miller, L. H., Green, J. R. (1970) 'Pattern-sensitive epilepsy, Part 1. An electrographic study of its mechanisms.' *Epilepsia*, **11**, 125.

—— —— —— —— —— Kupfer, C. (1970) 'Pattern sensitive epilepsy, Part 2. Clinical changes, tests of responsiveness and motor output, alterations of evoked potentials and therapeutic measures.' *Epilepsia*, **11**, 151.

Ciganek, L. (1961) 'The EEG response (evoked potential) to light stimulus in man.' *Electroencephalography and Clinical Neurophysiology*, **13**, 165.

Cobb, S. (1947) 'Photic driving as a cause of clinical seizures in epileptic patients.' *Archives of Neurology and Psychiatry*, **58**, 70.

Cobb, W. A., Morton, H. B., Ettlinger, G. (1967) 'Cerebral potentials evoked by pattern reversal and their suppression in visual rivalry.' *Nature*, **216**, 1123.

Cooper, J. E. (1965) 'Epilepsy in a longitudinal survey of 5000 children.' *British Medical Journal*, **i**, 1020.

Cooper, R., Osselton, J. W., Shaw, J. C. (1969) *EEG Technology*. London: Butterworths, p. 83.

Courjon, J. (1955) 'La protection des épileptiques photogéniques par des verres filtrant la partie rouge du spectre.' *Revue d'Oto-Neuro-Ophtalmologie*, **27**, 462.

Creutzfeldt, O. D., Kuhnt, U. (1967) 'The visual evoked potential: physiological, developmental and clinical aspects.' *Electroencephalography and Clinical Neurophysiology*, suppl. 26, 29.

—— Kugler, J., Morocutti, C., Sommer-Smith, J. A. (1966) 'Visual evoked potentials in normal human subjects and neurological patients.' *Electroencephalography and Clinical Neurophysiology*, **20**, 98.

Daly, D., Bickford, R. G. (1951) 'Electroencephalographic studies of identical twins with photo-epilepsy.' *Electroencephalography and Clinical Neurophysiology*, **3**, 245.

—— Siekert, R. G., Burke, E. C. (1959) 'A variety of familial light sensitive épilepsy.' *Electroencephalography and Clinical Neurophysiology*, **11**, 141.

Davidson, S., Watson, C. W. (1956) 'Hereditary light-sensitive epilepsy.' *Neurology*, **6**, 235.

Darby, C. E., Hindley, A. T. (1974) 'Electroencephalographic changes in photosensitive patients whilst watching television.' *Proceedings of the Electrophysiological Technologists' Association*, **21**, 4.

Dawson, G. D. (1951) 'A summation technique for detecting small signals in a large irregular background. (Proceedings of the Physiological Society).' *Journal of Physiology*, **115**, 2P.

—— (1954) 'A summation technique for the detection of small evoked potentials.' *Electroencephalography and Clinical Neurophysiology*, **6**, 65.

Dimitrakoudi, M., Harding, G. F. A., Jeavons, P. M. (1973) 'The inter-relation of the $P_2$ component of the V.E.R. with occipital spikes produced by patterned intermittent photic stimulation.' *Electroencephalography and Clinical Neurophysiology*, **35**, 416.

Doose, H., Gerken, H. (1973) 'Possibilities and limitations of epilepsy prevention in siblings of epileptic children.' *In* Parsonage, M. J. (Ed.) *Prevention of Epilepsy and its Consequences*. London: International Bureau for Epilepsy.

—— —— Hein-Völpei, K. F., Völzke, E. (1969a) 'Genetics of photosensitive epilepsy.' *Neuropädiatrie*, **1**, 56.

—— Giesler, K., Völzke, E. (1969b) 'Observations in photosensitive children with and without epilepsy.' *Zeitschrift für Kinderheilkunde*, **107**, 26.

Dustman, R. E., Beck, E. C. (1969) 'The effects of maturation and aging on the wave form of visually evoked potentials.' *Electroencephalography and Clinical Neurophysiology*, **26**, 2.

Dumermuth, G. (1961) 'Photosensible epilepsie und Television.' *Schweizerische medizinische Wochenschrift*, **91**, 1633.

Engel, J. (1974) 'Selective photoconvulsive responses to intermittent diffuse and patterned photic stimulation.' *Electroencephalography and Clinical Neurophysiology*, **37**, 283.

Ebe, M., Meier-Ewert, K.-H., Broughton, R. (1969) 'Effects of intravenous diazepam (Valium) upon evoked potentials of photosensitive epileptic and normal subjects.' *Electroencephalography and Clinical Neurophysiology*, **27**, 429.

—— Mikami, T., Ito, H., Aki, M., Miyazaki, M. (1963) 'Photically evoked potentials in brain disorders.' *Tohoku Journal of Experimental Medicine*, **80**, 323.

Forster, F. M. (1967) 'Conditioning of cerebral dysrhythmia induced by pattern presentation and eye closure.' *Conditional Reflex*, **2**, 236.

—— Campos, G. B. (1964) 'Conditioning factors in stroboscopic-induced seizures.' *Epilepsia*, **5**, 156.

—— Ptacek, L. J., Peterson, W. G. (1965) 'Auditory clicks in extinction of stroboscope-induced seizures.' *Epilepsia*, **6**, 217.

—— —— —— Chun, R. W. M., Bengson, A. R. A., Campos, G. B. (1964) 'Stroboscopic-induced seizure discharges. Modification by extinction techniques.' *Neurology*, **11**, 603.

Ganglberger, J. A., Cvetko, B. (1956) 'Photogene Epilepsie.' *Wiener Zeitschrift für Nervenheilkunde und deren Grenzgebiete*, **13**, 22.

Gastaut, H. (1950) 'Un signe électroencéphalographique des hydrocéphalies: la répouse par recrutement au cours de la stimulation lumineuse intermittente.' *Revue neurologique,* **82,** 410.
—— (1970) 'Clinical and electroencephalographical classification of epileptic seizures.' *Epilepsia,* **11,** 102.
—— (1973) *Dictionary of Epilepsy.* Geneva: World Health Organization.
—— Corriol, J. (1951) 'Note préliminaire sur un procédé nouveau et particulièrement efficace de stimulation lumineuse intermittente.' *Electroencephalography and Clinical Neurophysiology,* **3,** 87.
—— Franck, G., Krolikowska, W., Naquet, R., Roger, J. (1963) 'Phénomènes de déafferentation sensorielle spécifique décélés par l'enregistrement transcranien des potentiels évoqués visuels chez des sujets présentant des crises épileptiques visuelles dans leur champ hémianopsique uni-ou-bilatéral.' *Revue Neurologique,* **109,** 249.
—— Regis, H. (1964) 'Visually-evoked potentials recorded transcranially in man.' *In* Proctor, L. D., Adey, W. R. (Eds.) *Symposium on the Analysis of Central Nervous System and Cardiovascular Data Using Computer Methods.* Washington: NASA SP 72, p. 8.
—— —— Bostem, F. (1962) 'Attacks provoked by television and their mechanism.' *Epilepsia,* **3,** 438.
—— —— —— Beaussart, M. (1960) 'Etude électroencéphalographique de 35 sujets ayant présenté des crises au cours d'un spectacle télévisé.' *Revue Neurologique,* **102,** 553.
—— Roger, J., Corriol, J., Gastaut. Y. (1948) 'Les formes expérimentales de l'épilepsie humaine: L'épilepsie induite par la stimulation lumineuse intermittent rhythmée ou épilepsie photogénique.' *Revue Neurologique,* **80,** 161.
—— Tassinari, C. A. (1966) 'Triggering mechanisms in epilepsy. The electroclinical point of view.' *Epilepsia,* **7,** 85.
—— Trevisan, C., Naquet, R. (1958) 'Diagnostic value of electroencephalographic abnormalities provoked by intermittent photic stimulation.' *Electroencephalography and Clinical Neurophysiology,* **10,** 194.
Gerken, H., Doose, H., Völzke, E., Volz, C., Hien-Völpel, K. F. (1968) 'Genetics of childhood epilepsy with photic sensitivity.' *Lancet,* **1,** 1377.
Gibberd, F. B. (1966) 'The clinical features of petit mal.' *Acta Neurologica Scandinavica,* **42,** 176.
Goldstein, S. (1970) 'Phase coherence of the alpha rhythm during photic blocking.' *Electroencephalography and Clinical Neurophysiology,* **29,** 127.
Goodkind, R., (1936) 'Myoclonic and epileptic attacks precipitated by bright light.' *Archives of Neurology and Psychiatry (Chicago),* **35,** 868.
Gowers, W. R. (1885) *Epilepsy and Other Chronic Convulsive Diseases. Their Causes, Symptoms and Treatment.* New York: Wood & Co.
Green, J. B. (1966) 'Self-induced seizures.' *Archives of Neurology,* **15,** 579.
—— (1968) 'Seizures on closing the eyes. Electroencephalographic studies.' *Neurology,* **18,** 391.
—— (1969) 'Photosensitive epilepsy. The electroretinogram and visually evoked response.' *Archives of Neurology,* **20,** 191.
Gross, E. G., Vaughan, H. G., Valenstein, E. (1967) 'Inhibition of visual evoked responses to patterned stimuli during voluntary eye movements.' *Electroencephalography and Clinical Neurophysiology,* **22,** 204.
Haneke, K. (1963) 'Uber drei Fälle latenter und manifester photogener Epilepsie in einer Familie.' *Kinderärztliche Praxis,* **31,** 149.
Harding, G. F. A. (1974) 'The visual evoked response.' *In* Roper-Hall, M. J., Autter, H., Striff, E. B. (Eds.) *Advances in Ophthalmology,* **28,** 2. Basel: Karger.
—— Dimitrakoudi, M. 'The visual evoked response in photosensitive epilepsy.' In Desmedt, J. (Ed.) *Evoked Potentials in Man.* Oxford University Press. (In Press).
—— Drasdo, N., Kabrisky, M., Jeavons, P. M. (1969a) 'A proposed therapeutic device for photosensitive epilepsy.' *Proceedings of the Electrophysiological Technology Association,* **16,** 19.
—— Thompson, C. R. S., Panayiotopoulos, C. P. (1969b) 'Evoked responses diagnosis in visual field defects.' *Proceedings of the Electrophysiological Technology Association,* **16,** 159.
Harley, R. D., Baird, H. W., Freeman, R. D. (1967) 'Self-induced photogenic epilepsy. Report of four cases.' *Archives of Ophthalmology,* **78,** 730.
Harter, M. R., White, C. T., (1970) 'Evoked cortical responses to checkerboard patterns: effect of check-size as a function of visual acuity.' *Electroencephalography and Clinical Neurophysiology,* **28,** 48.
—— Salmon, L. E. (1971) 'Evoked cortical responses to patterned light flashes: effects of ocular convergence and accommodation.' *Electroencephalography and Clinical Neurophysiology,* **30,** 527.
Heintel, H. (1965) 'Photosensible Epilepsie und Fernsehen.' *Nervenartz,* **36,** 123.
Herrick, C. (1973) *The Inheritance of Photosensitivity.* Unpublished M.Sc. Dissertation. Birmingham University of Aston.
Herrlin, K. M. (1954) 'EEG with photic stimulation: a study of children with manifest or suspected epilepsy.' *Electroencephalography and Clinical Neurophysiology,* **6,** 573.

Hess, R. (1961) Electroencephalography and Cerebral Tumours. *Electroencephalography and Clinical Neurophysiology,* suppl. 19, 98.

Hishikawa, Y., Yamamoto, J., Furuya, E., Yamada, Y., Miyazaki, K., Kaneko, Z. (1967) 'Photosensitive epilepsy: relationships between the visual evoked responses and the epileptiform discharges induced by intermittent photic stimulation.' *Electroencephalography and Clinical Neurophysiology,* 23, 320.

Holmes, G. (1927) 'Epilepsy a cerebral disease.' *Lancet,* ii, 554.

Hubel, D. H., Wiesel, T. N. (1962) 'Receptive fields, binocular interaction and functional architecture in the cat's visual cortex.' *Journal of Physiology,* 160, 106.

—— —— (1965) 'Receptive fields and functional architecture in two non-striate visual areas (18 and 19) of the cat.' *Journal of Neurophysiology,* 28, 229.

—— —— (1968) 'Receptive fields and functional architecture of monkey striate cortex.' *Journal of Physiology,* 195, 215.

Hughes, J. R. (1960) 'Usefulness of photic stimulation in routine clinical electroencephalography.' *Neurology,* 10, 777.

Hull, C. L. (1943) *Principles of Behaviour.* New York: Appleton-Century.

Hutchison, J. H., Stone, F. H., Davidson, J. R. (1958) 'Photogenic epilepsy induced by the patient.' *Lancet,* i, 243.

Ismay, G. (1958) 'Photogenic epilepsy.' *Lancet,* i, 376.

Jasper, H. H. (1958) 'The ten-twenty electrode system of the International Federation.' *Electroencephalography and Clinical Neurophysiology,* 10, 371.

Jeavons, P. M. (1966) 'Summary of paper on abnormalities during photic stimulation.' *Proceedings of the Electrophysiological Technology Association,* 13, 153.

—— (1969) 'The use of photic stimulation in clinical electroencephalography.' *Proceedings of the Electrophysiological Technology Association,* 16,225.

—— (1972) 'Clinics for the treatment of epilepsy and convulsions.' *Lancet,* i, 904.

—— Clarke, J. E. (1974) 'Sodium valproate in treatment of epilepsy.' *British Medical Journal,* ii, 584.

—— Harding, G. F. A. (1970) 'Television epilepsy.' *Lancet,* ii, 926.

—— —— Bower, B. D. (1966) 'Intermittent photic stimulation in photosensitive epilepsy.' *Electroencephalography and Clinical Neurophysiology,* 21, 308.

—— —— Panayiotopoulos, C. P. (1971) 'Photosensitive epilepsy and driving.' *Lancet,* i, 1125.

—— —— —— (1972) 'The effect of lateral gaze and lateral illumination on photoconvulsive responses to intermittent photic stimulation.' *Electroencephalography and Clinical Neurophysiology,* 33, 447.

—— —— —— Drasdo, N. (1972) 'The effect of geometric patterns combined with intermittent photic stimulation in photosensitive epilepsy.' *Electroencephalography and Clinical Neurophysiology,* 33, 221.

—— Maheshwari, M. C. (1974) 'The effect of Epilim on epilepsy and the EEG.' *Electroencephalography and Clinical Neurophysiology,* 37, 326.

Johnson, L. C. (1963) 'Flicker as a helicopter pilot problem.' *Aerospace Medicine,* 34, 306.

Jonkman, E. J. (1967) *The Average Cortical Response to Photic Stimulation.* Unpublished thesis. University of Amsterdam.

Keith, H. M. (1963) *Convulsive disorders in Children with Reference to Treatment with Ketogenic Diet.* Boston: Little, Brown.

Klapetek, J. (1959) 'Photogenic epileptic seizures provoked by television.' *Electroencephalography and Clinical Neurophysiology,* 11, 809.

Kooi, K. A. (1971) *Fundamentals of Electroencephalography.* New York: Harper and Row.

—— Eckman, H. G. Thomas, M. H. (1957) 'Observations on the response to photic stimulation in organic cerebral dysfunction.' *Electroencephalography and Clinical Neurophysiology,* 9, 239.

—— Thomas, M. H., Mortenson, F. N. (1960) 'Photoconvulsive and photomyoclonic responses in adults.' *Neurology,* 10, 1051.

Lagergren, J., Hansson, B. (1960) 'Television epilepsy.' *Journal of the American Medical Association,* 172, 475.

Laget, P., Humbert, R. (1954) 'Facteurs influencant la réponse électroencéphalographique à la photostimulation chez l'enfant.' *Electroencephalography and Clinical Neurophysiology,* 6, 591.

Le Grand, Y. (1968) *Light, Colour and Vision.* London: Chapman and Hall.

Lennox, W. G. (1960) *Epilepsy and Related Disorders.* London: Churchill.

Livingston, S. (1952) 'Comments on a study of light-induced epilepsy in children.' *American Journal of Diseases of Children,* 83, 409.

—— Pruce, I. M. (1972) *Comprehensive Management of Epilepsy in Infancy, Childhood and Adolescence.* Springfield, Ill.: C. C. Thomas.

115

—— Torres, I. C. (1964) 'Photic epilepsy: report of an unusual case and review of the literature.' *Clinical Pediatrics,* **3,** 304.

Lloyd-Smith, D. L., Henderson, L. R. (1951) 'Epileptic patients showing susceptibility to photic stimulation alone.' *Electroencephalography and Clinical Neurophysiology,* **3,** 378.

Loiseau, P., Cohadon, S. (1962) 'Trois cas d'épilepsie photosensible avec autoprovocation des crises.' *Revue Neurologique,* **107,** 231.

Lücking, C. H., Creutzfeldt, O. D., Heinemann, U. (1970) 'Visual evoked potentials of patients with epilepsy and of a control group.' *Electroencephalography and Clinical Neurophysiology,* **29,** 557.

Maheshwari, M. C., Jeavons, P. M. (1975) 'The clinical significance of occipital spikes as a sole response to intermittent photic stimulation.' *Electroencephalography and Clinical Neurophysiology,* **39,** 93.

Maruyama, K., Maruyama, H. (1968) 'Light sensitive epilepsy. Clinical and electroencephalographic studies on 74 cases, especially on EEG activation by television.' *Advances in Neurological Science,* **12,** 537.

Mawdsley, C. (1961) 'Epilepsy and television.' *Lancet,* **i,** 190.

Marshall, C., Walker, A. E., Livingston, S. (1953) 'Photogenic epilepsy; parameters of activation.' *Archives of Neurology and Psychiatry,* **69,** 760.

Meier-Ewert, K., Broughton, R. J. (1967) 'Photomyoclonic response of epileptic and non-epileptic subjects during wakefulness, sleep and arousal.' *Electroencephalography and Clinical Neurophysiology,* **23,** 142.

Melsen, S. (1959) 'The value of photic stimulation in the diagnosis of epilepsy.' *Journal of Nervous and Mental Diseases,* **128,** 508.

Metrakos, J. D., Metrakos, K. (1960) 'Genetics of convulsive disorders. I. Introduction, problems, methods and base lines.' *Neurology,* **10,** 228.

—— —— (1961) 'Genetics of convulsive disorders. Genetic and electroencephalographic studies in centrencephalic epilepsy.' *Neurology,* **11,** 474.

—— —— (1966) 'Childhood epilepsy of subcortical ('Centrencephalic') origin.' *Clinical Pediatrics,* **5,** 536.

—— —— (1969) 'Genetic studies in clinical epilepsy.' *In* Jasper, H. H., Ward, A. A., Pope, A. (Eds.) *Basic Mechanisms of the Epilepsies.* Boston: Little, Brown.

Morocutti, C., Sommer-Smith, J. A. (1966) 'Etude des potentiels évoqués visuels dans l'épilepsies.' *Revue Neurologique,* **115,** 93.

—— —— Creutzfeldt, O. (1964) 'Studio dei potenziali evocati visivi in soggetti normali ed in soggetti affetti da malattia cerebrali.' *Rivista di Neurologia,* **34,** 57.

Mundy-Castle, A. C. (1953) 'Clinical significance of photic stimulation.' *Electroencephalography and Clinical Neurophysiology,* **5,** 187.

Needham, W. E., Dustman, R. E., Bray, P. F., Beck, E. C. (1971) 'Intelligence, EEG, and visual evoked potentials in centrencephalic epilepsy.' *Electroencephalography and Clinical Neurophysiology,* **30,** 94.

Pallis, C., Louis, S. (1961) 'Television-induced seizures.' *Lancet,* **i,** 188.

Panayiotopoulos, C. P. (1972) A Study of Photosensitive Epilepsy with particular reference to occipital Spikes induced by Intermittent Photic Stimulation. Unpublished thesis. Birmingham: University of Aston.

—— (1974) 'Effectiveness of photic stimulation on various eye-states in photosensitive epilepsy.' *Journal of the Neurological Sciences,* **23,** 165.

—— Jeavons, P. M., Harding, G. F. A. (1970) 'Relation of occipital spikes evoked by intermittent photic stimulation to visual evoked responses in photosensitive epilepsy.' *Nature,* **228,** 566.

—— —— —— (1972) 'Occipital spikes and their relation to visual evoked responses in epilepsy, with particular reference to photosensitive epilepsy.' *Electroencephalography and Clinical Neurophysiology,* **32,** 179.

Pantelakis, S. N., Bower, B. D., Jones, H. D. (1962) 'Convulsions and television viewing.' *British Medical Journal,* **ii,** 633.

Parsons-Smith, G. (1953) 'Flicker stimulation in amblyopia.' *British Journal of Ophthalmology,* **37,** 424.

Petersen, I., Eeg-Olofsson, O., Sellden, U, (1968) 'Paroxysmal activity in EEG of normal children.' *In* Kellaway, P., Petersen, I. (Eds.) *Clinical Electroencephalography of Children.* Stockholm: Almqvist and Wiksell, pp. 167.

Pond, D. A., Bidwell, B. H., Stein, L. (1960) 'A survey of epilepsy in fourteen general practices. I. Demographic and medical data.' *Psychiatria, Neurologia, Neurochirurgia,* **63,** 217.

Rabending, G., Krell, D., Parnitzke, K. H. (1967) 'Der Einfluss der Photostimulation auf die Herzschlagfolge.' *Deutsche Zeitschrift für Nervenheilkunde,* **192,** 139.

Radovici, A., Misirliou, V., Gluckman, M. L. (1932) 'Epilepsy réflexe provoquée par excitations optiques des rayons solaires.' *Revue Neurologique,* **1,** 1305.

116

Rao, K. S., Prichard, J. S. (1955) 'Photogenic epilepsy.' *Journal of Pediatrics*, **47**, 619.
Richter, H. R. (1960) 'Télévision et épilepsie.' *Revue Neurologique*, **103**, 283.
Rieth, A. (1960) *5000 Jahre Topferscheibe*. Konstanz: Thorbecke.
Rivano, C., Rossi, G. F., Siani, C., Zattoni, J. (1968) 'The suppressive effect of Mogadon on photo-induced epilepsy.' Amsterdam: Excerpta Medica, **193**, (152).
Robertson, E. G. (1954) 'Photogenic epilepsy; self-precipitated attacks.' *Brain*, **77**, 232.
Rodin, E. A., Daly, D. D., Bickford, R. G. (1955) 'Effects of photic stimulation during sleep. A study of normal subjects and epileptic patients.' *Neurology*, **5**, 149.
Rossi, G. F., Frank, L., Pazzaglia, P. (1969) 'Crisi epilettiche alla chiusura degli occhi.' *Giornale di Psichiatria e di Neuropatologia*, **97**, 469.
Rutter, M., Graham, P., Yule, W. (1970) *A Neuropsychiatric Study in Childhood*. Clinics in Developmental Medicine no. 35/36. London: S.I.M.P./Heinemann.
Schwartz, J. F. (1962) 'Photosensitivity in a family.' *American Journal of Diseases of Children*, **103**, 786.
Scollo-Lavizzari, G. (1971) 'Prognostic significance of "epileptiform" discharges in the EEG of non-epileptic subjects during photic stimulation.' *Electroencephalography and Clinical Neurophysiology*, **31**, 174.
Shagass, C. (1954) 'Clinical significance of the photomyoclonic response in psychiatric patients.' *Electroencephalography and Clinical Neurophysiology*, **6**, 445.
Spehlmann, R. (1965) 'The averaged electrical responses to diffuse and to patterned light in the human.' *Electroencephalography and Clinical Neurophysiology*, **19**, 560.
Spekreijse, H. (1966) *Analysis of EEG Responses in Man Evoked by Sine Wave Modulated Light*. The Hague: W. Junk.
Spilker, B., Kamiya, J., Calloway, T., Yeager, C. (1969) 'Visual evoked responses in subjects trained to control alpha rhythm.' *Psychophysiology*, **5**, 683.
Storm van Leeuwen, W., Bekkering, D. H. (1958) 'Some results obtained with the EEG-spectrograph.' *Electroencephalography and Clinical Neurophysiology*, **10**, 563.
Temkin, O. (1971) *The Falling Sickness*. 2nd ed. Baltimore/London: Johns Hopkins Press.
Troupin, A. S. (1966) 'Photic activation and experimental data concerning colored stimuli.' *Neurology*, **16**, 269.
Turton, E. C. (1952) 'An electronic trigger used to assist in the EEG diagnosis of epilepsy.' *Electroencephalography and Clinical Neurophysiology*, **4**, 83.
Ulett, G. A., Johnson, L. C. (1958) 'Pattern, stability and correlates of photic electroencephalographic activation.' *Journal of Nervous and Mental Diseases*, **126**, 153.
van der Tweel, L. H., Spekreijse, H. (1966) 'Visual evoked responses.' *In* Francois, J. (Ed.) *The Clinical Value of Electroretinography*, ISCERG Symposium. Basel: Karger, p. 83.
Völzke, E., Doose, H. (1973) 'Dipropylacetate (Dépakine, Ergenyl) in the treatment of epilepsy.' *Epilepsia*, **14**, 185.
Wadlington, W. B., Riley, H. D. (1965) 'Light-induced seizures. *Journal of Pediatrics*, **66**, 300.
Walter, V. J., Walter, W. G. (1949) 'The central effects of rhythmic sensory stimulation.' *Electroencephalography and Clinical Neurophysiology*, **1**, 57.
—— (1961) *The Living Brain*. Harmondsworth: Penguin Books, p. 91.
—— Dovey, V. J., Shipton, H. (1946) 'Analysis of the electrical response of the human cortex to photic stimulation.' *Nature*, **158**, 540.
Watson, C., Davidson, S. (1957) 'The pattern of inheritance of cerebral light sensitivity.' *Electroencephalography and Clinical Neurophysiology*, **9**, 378.
Watson, C. W., Marcus, E. M. (1962) 'The genetics and clinical significance of photogenic cerebral electrical abnormalities myoclonus and seizures.' *Transactions of the American Neurological Association*, **87**, 251.

# List of Figures

# Subject Index

Bold type = Tables
Italic = Figures